The Mysterious and Secret Order Of The Knights Of The Golden Circle

By

Dr. Roy William Roush, Ph.D

Published by Front Line Press

Copyright March 2005
ISBN: 0-9723072-6-5

Printed in the United States of America

Copies of this book can be ordered from the Website
Knightsofthegoldencircle.net or by Phone (818) 888-5416

All rights reserved. No part of this book may be used, reproduced, photocopied, stored in any retrieval system, recorded, or transmitted by any means whatsoever without written permission from the author or publisher, except for brief quotes or excerpts for reviews, provided proper credit is given.

ABOUT THIS BOOK

This is an incredible story about the little known and secret order of "The Knights of the Golden Circle" during the Civil War period, their plans to start another war, and the huge treasures they left behind. But, they had started many years before the war began with bold plans of imperialism to gain more territory for our growing nation (which brought Texas into the Union), and also with amazing plans to annex Mexico. Later, they became devout believers in the rights of the southern cause and against the North imposing it's will against them.

When the Civil War started, they resorted to drastic measures and went underground to oppose the North and the Union Army with secretive and bold actions, including sabotage, infiltration of the Government, and a very efficient spy network. Many top politicians, officials, and men of importance were members. They were so effective that President Lincoln once referred to them as a "Fifth Column" which might have been the original use of the term.

After the war was over, they refused to accept the terms of the surrender and started making plans to restart the war at a later date. But they needed a great amount of money and support. So they started collecting money, gold, silver, and jewelry, plus arms and ammunition, and buried them in many parts of the country in old mining tunnels, pits and holes that they dug, then assigned armed sentries to protect them from being found. But by the time they had amassed their fortune and supplies, World War One brought an end to their plans. Also, most of them had died off anyway by then. But the treasures they buried, which some have estimated to be worth billions of dollars, is the stuff that dreams are made of to treasure hunters.

The author, who is well-known in the field of treasure hunting, learned of this immense treasure years ago, and through his research has presented this information here--not only bringing out this little known part of American history, but also has provided much information on the treasures, including some rare and never-before-published treasure maps of some of the treasure sites.

Dedication

I dedicate this book to the memory of two of my very good friends and fellow treasure hunters who we lost in 2004: Gordon "Gordo" Cooper, one of the Original Seven Mercury Astronauts who set many world records in space and was the hottest fighter pilot I ever knew---and to Steve Ryland, owner of Cal-Gold and Pro-Mack-South treasure and gold prospecting shops, who I had worked with for many years and was my associate while writing the "Treasure Hunter Confidential Newsletter." And thanks to my wife, Lydia, for her patience while writing this book.

Other Credits of Dr. Roy William Roush

Author of *Open Fire*, a major 707-page story of personal, front line combat with the Marine Corps during the epic battles of Guadalcanal, Tarawa, Saipan and Tinian in the South Pacific during World War II. The book was awarded the "Best Non-fiction Book of 2004" by the Book Publists of Southern California. Author is also seen giving information about the combat being shown on the best selling video game *"Medal of Honor--The Rising Sun"* and *"The Assault on Tarawa"* by Electronic Arts Entertainments.

Author of: *Lost Treasure Secrets* and *Fugitives from Freedom*.

Columnist, feature story writer and staff member of: *Treasure, Treasure Search, Treasure Found, Treasure Diver, Treasure Hunter,* and *Treasure News*.

Co-editor and feature writer: *Treasure Hunter Confidential Newsletter*.

Contributing editor: *Biblical and American Archeologist Newsletter*.

Editor: *Adventure's Club News of Los Angeles*.

Columnist and reporter: *The Kansas City Star, Rocky Mountain Aviation Magazine, Fabulous Las Vegas Magazine, Stillwater News Press,* and the *O'Collegian*.

Technical writer for Aerospace Companies for 27 years.

Professor: UCLA and Los Angeles City Colleges.

Featured on *"Unsolved Mysteries"* Television Program, *"The Treasure of Elysian Park."*
Also on *"John Burrud's Treasure Series."*
On NBC's Special *"Treasure Hunting for the Spanish Treasure Galleons"* in Varacruz, Mexico.
On NBC's *"How to Find Treasure"* Series.
And on the Frank Sayer Show "The Lost Dutchman Mine."

Contents

About This Book
Dedication
Other Credits of Dr. Roy William Roush

INTRODUCTION
    Origins of the Knights of the Golden Circle 1
    Their Great Treasure Hoard 2

Chapt 1. THE HISTORY OF THE KNIGHTS OF THE GOLDEN CIRCLE 5
    Their Secret Organization 5
    Their Imperialists Plans and the Louisiana Purchase 5
    Texas 6
    Knights of the Golden Circle in California During the Civil War 7
    Their Amazing Plans to Invade Mexico 8
    Their Sworn Vows 11
    Their Preamble 18
    Their Obligation 19
    Conclusion 23
    Bibliography 24

Chapt 2. KNIGHTS OF THE GOLDEN CIRCLE--TREASON HISTORY, 1864 ... 25
    Unwritten Secret Work of The Order of Sons of Liberty 26
    Grips, Signs, Passwords, Etc. Never Before Published 27
    Explanation of the Initials used in the Rituals 31
    Rituals of the Order of Sons of Liberty - Neophyte or Vestibule Degree 32

Chapt. 3. JESSE JAMES III. THE MAN WHO SAID HE KNEW WHERE THE KNIGHTS BURIED THEIR TREASURES 35
    Jesse James III—The Great Grandson of Jesse James 36
    Was Jesse James Still Alive in Oklahoma in 1948? 36
    Who Was Really Buried in Jesse James's Grave? 37
    The Plot 38
    Jesse James III---Or Was He Really Frank Hawks? 39
    Treasure Maps 39

Chapt. 4. A TREASURE HUNT TO GLORIETA PASS, NEW MEXICO 70
    Some Clues 71
    The Discovery 73
    The Man Who Had Found the Treasure 75

Chapt. 5. DEL WRITES A BOOK, *JESSE JAMES WAS ONE OF HIS NAMES* . 89

Chapt. 6. A TREASURE HUNTERS CONVENTION IN TULSA, OKLAHOMA AND A VISIT TO KGC TERRITORY 107
    My Program on the KGC and Their Treasures 107
    A Treasure Trip to Southwestern Arkansas 108
    The Mysterious Treasure Signs. 109
    Armed KGC Sentinels Had Protected the Treasures 110
    The Bible Tree. 111

Chapt 7. WAS KGC TREASURE BURIED ON MY FATHERS OLD FARM IN KANSAS? 121
    The KGC Sentinel Who Had Threatened My Grandfather 123
    About the Author. 131

INTRODUCTION

Few people know of the Knights of the Golden Circle and even fewer know about the purpose for which it existed. It is probably the greatest untold story today in the history of the United States. That is unusual because during the last century this very large, powerful, secret, and subversive southern organization had such a profound influence and effect over the course of many years that they almost succeeded in changing the course of our history.

It has been said of them that they were one of the deadliest, wealthiest, most secretive and efficient spy and underground organizations in the history of the world. It is known that they operated not only in the United States, but also around the globe for 65 years (1851 to 1916). Also, that the original Ku Klux Klan was their military arm. Some of the finest and craftiest brains in the South helped organize and direct the activities of the Knights of the Golden Circle. The group was heavy on ritual, most of which was borrowed from the Masonic Lodge and later from the Knights of Pythias. Some were also members of the Rosicrucians. Their wealth was due to the huge amount of money, valuables and equipment that they had accumulated for the purpose of restarting the Civil War.

So, you might wonder then if that is true, why haven't we read about them in our history books or heard them mentioned in our schools before? That is a hard question to answer, but maybe because they were such devout, die-hard, southern rebels, working for a southern cause that was eventually defeated and one that is not popular today. However, the fact remains that since they did exist and were a very large and powerful organization for many years, I think that their story should be known today.

But during the 1800's, many stories and articles did appear about the Knights of the Golden Circle in many newspapers, magazines and periodicals, before, during, and after the Civil War. But somehow, these stories have been overlooked or purposely omitted from our modern-day history books. So, who were the Knights of the Golden Circle and what was their purpose?

ORIGINS OF THE KNIGHTS OF THE GOLDEN CIRCLE

Actually, their beginning goes back to a long period before the Civil War when our young nation was reaching out for more territory. They were part of the overall imperialist's movement to expand our borders westward, even though they had not officially taken on the name of the Knights of the Golden Circle. Then, when the issue of slavery began to divide the sentiments of our country, they started to support the Southern states in trying to keep slavery alive because most of them were Southerners. As the issue of slavery finally divided the Union and the Civil War began, they became ardent supporters of the southern cause. This is when the organization became secret and went underground in their efforts to aid the Confederacy. Since they were considered subversive, that is why they became a secret organization. President Lincoln once referred to their very effective efforts against the North, as a "Fifth Column." That could have been the origination of the term.

Then, after the war was over, they refused to accept the terms of the southern surrender. They had been working diligently for many years to accomplish their goals and were not about to give them up. They had too much momentum going. Also, they were still bitter over the issue of slavery and of not establishing a Confederate nation independent from the northern states. This is when they went underground with a strongly determined and clandestine, even bizarre, plan to eventually restart the Civil War at a later time.

THEIR GREAT TREASURE HOARD

One of the things they needed to accomplish this was to first, be well supplied and equipped. That is when they began to collect money, jewelry, gold, silver, and other valuable items from sympathizers to finance their cause. Many believe that they started out with what was left of the Confederate treasury at the end of the war. Treasure hunters have been looking for years for the missing wagon loads of gold that belonged to the Confederates as it was being moved that was never found. Additionally, they collected guns, ammunition, armament, uniforms, and other items to supply an army. This was the start of their huge treasure trove when they began to hide these items in mines and tunnels throughout the country, then covering the entrance. In other places, holes and huge tunnels were dug, items buried, then cleverly concealed. That happened mostly in the southern part of the United States, especially in the Southeast.

Amazing…unbelievable…ridiculous! Of course, it may sound that way, but who they were and what they did is a matter of record that is substantiated in many newspaper articles and other publications during the 1800's and later.

History was one of my favorite subjects during my school years (starting in the 1930's) and later during college and while earning a Ph.D. in archaeology. Yet, nothing was ever mentioned about the Knights of the Golden Circle. I have been heavily involved in hunting for lost treasures and mines for many years, and this is when I first heard about the Knights of the Golden Circle and the huge treasure caches they buried throughout the United States following the Civil War with the intent to restart the war again at a later date and a time when they had amassed enough resources to be successful with their daring venture.

During the 1970's, a few stories began to appear in some of the treasure publications giving some details about the amazing treasures of the Knights of the Golden Circle. If this were so, then I would have to classify it as America's greatest treasure and something that I would have to seriously investigate.

During this time period, I was also working on the staff of our most notable treasure publications, including: *Treasure Magazine, Treasure Search, Treasure Found, Treasure Hunter,* and *Treasure Diver* as the technical consultant and feature storywriter. I also wrote the "Question and Answer Columns." Some of the questions that readers would ask were for information on the Knights of the Golden Circle treasures. That forced me to begin a research project on this amazing subject matter.

In the next chapter, let's look at what has been recorded about the history of this astonishing organization and the important part they played in our history during the last century.

Chapter One

The History of the Knights of the Golden Circle

THEIR SECRET ORGANIZATION

The Knights of the Golden Circle (KGC) were formerly organized in 1835 as a secret organization by Senator John C. Calhoun, William Porcher and others, but their ideals had been going on for a number of years. The Knights of the Golden Circle were a direct descendent of other similar and secret societies, including one called The Lone Star. These men were southerners and their goal was the dissolution of the Union and to establish a Southern Empire--not a Confederacy or a Republic, but an Empire. It meant to achieve this purpose through a secret, large, and powerful organization, which indeed, they became.

In 1862, Charles G. Leyland wrote on page 573 in the Continental Monthly, "Nearly every man of influence in the South (and many a pretended Union man of the North) is a member of the Knights of the Golden Circle, and sworn, under the penalty of assassination, to labor, in season and out of season, by fair means or foul, at all times, and on all occasions, for accomplishments of its objective."

The article went on to explain that it was solely by means of their secret but powerful machinery that the southern states were plunged into revolution in defiance of the will of the majority of their voting population of the South. Open defiance of the Constitution of the United States was nothing unusual at that time in the South.

THEIR IMPERIALIST PLANS AND THE LOUISIANA PURCHASE

But actually, the Knights had their roots much earlier in our history-- going as far back as our 13 colonies when the desire to become an independent new nation from England arose. When that goal was achieved, a strong new spirit took hold, which was to grow even bigger and become more powerful. Flushed with success and with a strong sense of nationalistic pride, our founding fathers turned their eyes towards the West. They envisioned that some day, all of the territory up to the Mississippi River would become part of the United States, even though at the time, it was owned by France. Then surprisingly, that opportunity came in 1803 during the Napoleonic wars when Napoleon badly needed cash to continue his war against England and the Louisiana Purchase was made, selling all of the land east of the Mississippi to the United States. It was territory that was filled rather quickly by American settlers.

By then, the issue of slavery began to be a growing national problem and the sentiments between the North and the South began to divide our nation and threatened it with Civil War...the Southerners not wanting to give up slavery and the North opposing slavery. A Federal law to ban slavery could not be passed because of the opposition from the South. The Southerners, realizing that they were at a disadvantage in population and territory wanted to increase their odds and influence, but how?

TEXAS

The answer soon presented itself...Texas! But of course, that was in Mexican territory. However, the Mexican government, as early as 1812, wanted the vast open expanse of Texas settled, partly to gain more control over the hostile Indian population there. They had made a generous offer to anyone, even Americans, willing to go there and settle on a plot of land. So Americans, mostly from the South but many from Kentucky and Tennessee, went to the territory that became Texas and many took their slaves with them. Now, the southern states felt they had the support of a new neighbor, and in fact, they did. Of course, the issue of slavery had always been an issue from its beginnings in our country. Even though some northerners did own slaves, the use of slaves were not too useful in the growing industrial power of the North because they needed education and training to work in the factories. On the other hand, in the agricultural South, they were ideal for working in the fields. The South depended heavily from the benefit of slavery and was absolutely unwilling to give them up.

Whether the Southerners realized early-on that expanding slavery into this new territory and then capitalizing on the idea by encouraging Americans, especially Southerners, to go there with their slaves, may be a matter of conjecture, but I feel confident that they realized it was too good of an opportunity to pass up and certainly did just that, especially since they knew it was adjoining our new territory gained by the Louisiana Purchase, and that if enough Americans went there with slaves, they would probably want to join the United States later, obviously as a slaveholding state.

This conjecture can be substantiated by the fact that in 1826, a rebellion broke out in Texas, led mostly by the Americans. Soon it led to open warfare and the famous battle of the Alamo in 1836. The Texans then organized an army into which many Americans, mostly Southerners, went to join their fellow Americans. This army, led by General Sam Houston, eventually defeated the Mexican Army, and in 1836, Texas declared itself an independent country. But that did not last for long, and not surprisingly, in 1845, they joined the Union of the United States as a slave state, even though the use of slaves in Texas was not wide spread.

In the mean-time, sentiments and animosity between the North and the South had grown stronger, and in 1835 it eventually led to the formalized and secret organization of the Knights of the Golden Circle to oppose the North in any way they could, and they were to have a significant impact on the course of action for the South.

THE KNIGHTS OF THE GOLDEN CIRCLE IN CALIFORNIA DURING THE CIVIL WAR

<u>**NOTE: The following information on the KGC was taken (as written) from The San Bernardino County Museum Association Quarterly, Volume XV, No. 4, Summer, 1968; and is reprinted here by permission in order to enlighten the reader of their long history and ideologies. It serves as a typical example of their nature, determination and how well entrenched they were around the country.**</u>

"The major purpose of this paper is to trace the development of the significant, yet little known, organization of the Knights of the Golden Circle (KGC) and its part in the Civil War. While the present work is primarily concerned with the group and its activities in California, it seems important that the reader have an adequate background into the KGC's earlier activities and structural organization. Also, it is hoped that by tracing the group from its earliest conception with its aims and various degrees of work the reader will have a better understanding of the problems involved with such an organization in California.

From its first inception the KGC was bent on empire building, and a pattern of conquest was charted for Mexico as early as 1835. The trained troops for this operation were of necessity drilled in secret as they were not part of any given government body. When, however, it was found that the mounting strife between the North and the South could not be resolved peacefully, plans for the taking of Mexico were dropped, and the members moved to those areas where they could do the most good--be it by subversion or actual warfare. Thus it was that California came into the picture.

California, along with a few other states at the beginning of the war, was neutral in its participation. It was to these states that the Knights came in force with but one aim in mind--to swing in the state to the South, or failing in this, to keep the state neutral. Californians seem to be receptive to the plan of the KGC.

THEIR PLANS TO INVADE MEXICO

The most significant yet little known organizations that worked most efficiently for the South during the Civil War was the KGC. This ultra-secret organization can, in a great sense, be blamed for the serious setbacks suffered by the North during the opening campaigns of the war. Well-trained and schooled in the art of what is now termed "fifth columnism," the KGC created havoc in the Northern and Western states.

Originally planned as a filibustering society to be used in Mexico, the order found a ready field in the North just prior to and during the outbreak of hostilities. Having as its goal, a scheme that was much bigger than it appeared on the surface, this organization was set up for empire building.

Their plan to establish an empire in Mexico was, to say the least, a grandiose plan. However, the methods to be employed in carrying out such an ambitious plan were involved with such painstaking care that they could easily be implemented and proved more than just a mere bit of talk. The Southerners had developed an army within the U.S. Army to assure themselves of the support needed to carry out such plans.

Although these operations had been formulated for some time, it was not until 1860 that they were known to the Southern populace by George W. Bickley, president of the KGC. In the course of the four-day convention of the Knights held at Riley, North Carolina, May 7-11, Bickley stated his plans publicly:

'Fellow Citizens of the Southern States. The object of the following pages is to fairly and honestly canvas the claims of the KGC organization to your respect full consideration and unprejudiced sympathy. The Knights of the Golden Circle constitutes a military organization as a nucleus around which to hang such political considerations, which will, if well managed, lend to the disenthrallment of the Cotton States from the oppressive majority of the manufacturing and commercial interest of the North.

It would also go to Mexico in the character of a Defensive Colony, and become a center, drawing to itself every good citizen who desires relief from the anarchy and civil wars which have so devastated that country since 1824. It would give protection to life and property, and rigidly enforce those great principles of sobriety and industry which had been so distinguishing a future in the rise in progress of Anglo-Americanism on this continent. But the KGC means to obey the laws of the United States as well on those of Mexico, and to avoid a single act which would bring a blush of shame to our cheeks. As Americans, we would Americanize Mexico for the common glory of our American character, and because the interest of the nation, no matter how viewed, demand such an accomplishment by our people. As Southern men, we would Americanize the country because therein rests the only hope of keeping cotton states of the Union on a footing of political equality with other states. As philanthropist, we would settle and Americanize Mexico, because the happiness of the people would be enhanced; and as Knights of the Golden Circle we would colonize and Americanize that country, we thereby open new avenues by which to benefit ourselves, financially, socially and religiously."

The speaker then turned from the topic at hand to trace the development of the breach between the North and the South, bringing out the vast differences, economically, politically, and socially; and blaming the North in all instances for having caused the mounting strife. He then returned to the original topic and placed another point before the people with which to strengthen his major premises for supporting the KGC in their master plan of empire building:

'Under these circumstances, the KGC would go forth and plant new colonies, build up new markets, and expand the area of Anglo-Americanism. We would educate our young men to the science of arms. We would acquire and hold as a rallying point and an outlet, other territories adapted to slave labor. We would remove the coming struggle between the North and South to the plains and valleys of Mexico. We would take the young man away from his dissipations and point him to the glittering crown of glory that awaits the brave and industrious. We would have such an organization in every Slave State that the nucleus would be ever present. Now fellow citizens of the South, we ask if the time has not arrived, if the exigencies of the times do not call for a powerful effort on the part of the people of the South to arrest this Northern policy which must soon lead to the most deplorable results?'

Bickley then attempted to justify the South's reasons for needing to take over Mexico by pointing out the anarchy that had existed there since 1824, and how it endangered Southern citizens in that country.

'Common humanity calls on us as a civilized people to arrest this state of anarchy and misrule. The Knights of the Golden Circle in cooperation with the best and only reliable people in Mexico have undertaken to infuse such an American element in that country as will lead to the establishment of a permanent and just government--if the threatening aspects of politics in our country and the disorganized condition in Mexico do not lead to the conclusion that the powers of the North in the South need balancing, and that Mexico is the weight to be thrown in the scales, then we are laboring under a wild and foolish delusion.

Under proper conditions, Mexico is the legitimate field of operations and Knights of the Golden Circle and hence some description of the country, its people, and their condition, must be more or less of interest to the Southern public. The relations of Mexico, either physically or politically considered to the commercial and political interests of the South, are strongly marked and worthy of serious attention."

At this point, Bickley unfolded the plan of the KGC for the aggrandizement of its commercial interest.

'We all look forward to the opening of new commercial relations and avenues to the acquirement of wealth; hence we contemplate a vast trade with China, Japan, and all of the Pacific Isles, which, to follow the natural channel, must cross Mexico on the line of the Old India Trade--from Acapulco to Vera Cruz, via the city of Mexico, and thence to New Orleans, Mobile, and Pensacola, to be distributed to the rest of the States of the Union, and even to the Canada's and Europe. To secure these advantages for the South, the Gulf of Mexico must be commanded, which can only be done by owning Mexico and the West Indies, or the principal of that group. This would not only give us the disbursement of that trade, but the whole commercial advantages of the Mississippi and its tributary valleys. That an enormous trade must be established between the Gulf States and what is now the Mexican Republic, the Western or Pacific States of America and the South of Asia and Polynesia will hardly be denied, and the sooner Mexico is Americanized, the sooner that trade will be established.'

Bickley next went on to explain other potential reasons for the Americanization of Mexico and the West Indies by pointing out that, if an army of 15,000 Knights of the Golden Circle invaded and took Vera Cruz, enough excitement would be caused to divert the attention of the United States from its sectional strife and the possibility of civil war. He also explained that the acquiring of the territory would increase the number of slave states of the South by about twenty-five. This would mean 50 more senators and about 60 more representatives for the South and the Congress of the United States.

Concerning the slave question, the plan stated: We would not draw slaves from the present slave states; but we would organize and remedy the defeats of the present Peon system of Mexico, and adapt the apprentice system of England, the old system of Brazil, and protect by law all Africans landed on our shores.

Bickley then proceeded to explain the organizational part of the KGC; but he seems to have his dates concerning its formation mixed up. He also gives credit erroneously to five members whom he names.

'The organization of the KGC is simple, yet we believe well adapted to the ends in view. It was originated at Lexington, Kentucky, on the fourth day of July 1854, by five gentleman who came together on a call made by General George Bickley, the president of the American Legion KGC. Only two of the five organizing members had survived to the present time. A clause in the fourth article of the obligations states, 'I will never desert the order of its arms as long as five brothers can be found who will remain true to its work, and in case of the death of our chief officer, I will, in concert with my brother Knights who have our sacred word and duguard (the sign given by the Masons and other fraternal societies) proceed to elect by a majority vote a successor to the said President, and such successor shall vow to carry out the true objects of this confederation of knighthood.'

THEIR SWORN VOWS

The third-degree has been given to but few persons, and to show that the gentleman who assumes its responsibilities were in earnest when they took the vows, we beg to quote from the degree work the prayer which each had repeated on bended knee, before taking those vows:

'O God, the creator of all things, incline us to wisdom and virtue. Protect and guard us, O King of Kings, against hypocrisy and deceit. Solemnly impress us, omnipotent God, that they are but men, and must give an honest account of every thought and deed unto thee. Prepare us to fulfill all the duties we are taking on ourselves, and make us as we professed to be, brothers indeed. Make us better men, wiser and more trustworthy, and deliver us from every temptation that may be cast in our way to cause us to violate our solemn vows. Hear and protect us, O father, as thy sons working for the glory of thy name, and the common good of our fellow men: make us true and faithful in all our duties to one another, and when danger threatens us, do thou be our shield in our defense--and as Christ suffered death for us, so incline us to die for one another. And now Master, be with us in our meeting; conduct us safely through life, and finally bring us to thy kingdom, full of honor and glory, for Christ's sake, Amen."

The men who pledged themselves to die by their institution, and whose hearts had been prepared for calm reflection by the above prayer, would not likely take any rash steps. And the organization of the KGC clearly shows that there was a very considerable amount of intellect employed in arranging the scheme. It is divided into three prominent divisions, and these divisions are again divided into classes, while again the classes are divided into departments.

There is the first division, which is absolutely a Military Degree, appealingly strongly to the chivalry and martial pride of our people. It is divided into two classes, the foreign and the home guards. The first is composed of such worthy and eligible men as wish to participate in wild, glorious and thrilling adventures of a campaign in Mexico, and who constitute the active army of the KGC. The second class, or home guard, embraces such members of the first degree of division, as are over-age for active duty, or who are from disease or deformity, incapacitated for military duty, and such ministers, lawyers, judges, officials, merchants and aged gentleman as are willing to assist and who sympathizes with the order, but can not from circumstances participate. In this home guard there are many of the first men of the South, and a large number of ladies of wealth and respectability--for Southern ladies are admitted to the first and second degree, but not to the third. The first of these classes--the Foreign Guard, is divided into all departments of a well-organized army. The second class--the Home Guard, has but two functions, viz: to assist in raising means for the provision of material and transportation of the army, and to defend us from misrepresentation during our absence. They know all that transpires, or that is contemplated, and enjoy certain renumerative advantages and privileges that may not here be explained.

The Second Division or degree is also divided into classes, the Foreign and the Home Corps, each of which has its special duties. This is the commercial and financial division; the Foreign Corps becomes settlers, commercial agents, paymasters, postmasters, clerks, physicians, ministers, teachers, editors, hunters, negotiators, etc. the Home Corps assist by their advice, and exertions, and contributions in getting money, arms, ammunition, clothing and other necessary material, and in forwarding the same to the army, and in assisting to direct public sentiment in proper channels, and in sending on recruits as fast as needed.

The Third Division or degree is also divided into two classes, the Foreign and Home Councils. This is the political or governing division. The "Home Council" is one of pure advisement, and takes no active steps. It is unknown to the public or the First Division of the KGC and is intended to guard us against infractions of the law. Like other Home classes it enjoys advantages known only to the order. The Foreign Council is divided into ten departments, representing respectively the interests of agriculture, education, manufactur- ing, finance, religion, police, war, navigation, and foreign relations. Also from the Foreign Council there is [sic] selected three classes as a high court of appeals entrusted with making laws for the government of the KGC. These classes represent respectively the interests of capital, manufacturing and mining interests, and the interests of commerce and agriculture.

The army is composed of four divisions of four thousand men each. Each division has four regiments and each regiment ten companies. There is one Major General, four Brigadier Generals, sixteen Colonels and sixteen Lieutenant Colonels, thirty-two Majors, and one hundred and sixty

Captains and their company officers, besides staff and department officers. The pay of the army and departments is one-eighth more than the salaries of the U.S. Army. For those of privates who settle in the country, 640 acres of land or $400 in money. Pensions are provided for those who may be disabled. The rations and clothing are ample. The land for officers is proportioned to rank.

Volunteers who are not members of the KGC, if of worthy characters, when presented in companies of over sixty-four, are accepted, if delivered at our camp in Texas, say Brownsville, free of cost for six, twelve, or eighteen months service, as they may prefer. They must be armed and uniformed—otherwise necessarily provided. Their pay will be the same as that of the army of the KGC. Their land donations will be one half for six and twelve months volunteers, and the same for those who serve eighteen months. No pensions are now provided for volunteer troops, but we hope to provide such. Those wishing to enlist as volunteers, must apply to the President or the Legion at Knoxville, Tennessee.

The membership now numbers nearly 48,000, though the army numbers less than 14,000 men strong. However, accretions are being daily received, and it is not to much to say that we could muster 100,000 men as easy as 20,000 if we could provide the money to put them in the field.

A gentleman desiring to be a KGC, and to organize a castle, will address a note to the President of the Legion of the KGC (Gen. Geo. Bickley) at Knoxville, Tennessee, enclosing evidence of his standing and character, when the form of an obligation will be sent to him, which he will fill out and acknowledge before a magistrates, or notary public, and return, and enclose with it the sum of five dollars whereupon the following castle works and papers will be at once forwarded:

    7 First Degree Books and 7 Keys
    7 Second Degree Books and 7 Keys
    2 Copies of Instructions
    1 Roll Book
    1 Set Receipts
    20 Copies of KGC Address
    1 Copy Rules and Regulations and such other papers as are needed.

Or, application may be made to any Colonel of the order, and the money may to be forwarded to him, whereupon he will order the papers. The works themselves will give all other information. Others who wish to loan or contribute money, will also apply to the President of the Legion at Knoxville, Tennessee, and he will forward the name of the Banking Agent in that State who will receive and receipt for the same; or the money may be forwarded to the Chairman of the Financial Bureau, General N. J. Scott, Auburn, Alabama, who will also receipt for the same.

To summarize the major points of his speech, Bickley continued: "Now, fellow-citizens, let us sum up and as Southern men, reason together. The KGC is a Southern Institution--the counteracting power of the Emigrant Aid Societies of the North. It is a lawful company, looking to the winning of Empire for the South. Also:

It would show an outlet for the free Negro population of the Southern States.

It would gain the control of the Gulf of Mexico and the vast trade thereof.

It would keep Mexico out of the hands of the Republican majority of the North.

It would make the South strong in or powerful out of the Union.

It would cultivate the martial spirit of our people and so tie together all the Southern States that if one secedes, all would go.

It would provide a vanguard in the great army of the South, which must be, at no distant day, brought in the field.

It would give peace and permanency to society in Mexico. It would protect the weak and punish the bad.

It would anticipate the North in the settlement of Mexico.

It would give the trade of Mexico to our own merchants.

It would plant our religion and civilization firmly in Mexico. We affiliate with the people, and labor with them against the anarchy and oppression to which they have been subject for a quarter of a century."

Very little has been known about the degree the work of this organization; however, some enlightening works have been uncovered. One, and probably the only one, actually dealing with the work of each individual degree is "A True Disclosure and Exposition of the Knights of the Golden Circle" written by J.W. Pomfrey in 1861. The brevity of this paper however does not allow the writer to expand upon the works, nor ceremony of these degrees.

The members of the aforesaid degrees, just prior to the out-break of hostilities between the North and the South, were switched from their original goal of Southern Empire building to infiltrate the Northern and Western states. Before long, it became apparent that these thoroughly organized workers were doing their jobs well in the states to which they had been sent.

Speaking in the Senate on December 12, 1859, William M. Gwin of Tennessee, declared that he believed that all slave holding states of the confederacy can establish a separate and independent government that will be impregnable to the assaults of all foreign enemies. He further went on to show that they had the power to do it, and asserted that if the southern states went out of the Union, California would fight with the South.

Add to this the many other potential dangers that were rippling the surface and it is easy to see that the crisis in California was a reality--not just rumor--for, if ever a state were divided in its sentiment, it was California at the beginning of the Civil War.

About three-eighths of the population were of southern descent and solidly united in sympathy for the Confederate states. This vigorous minority included upwards of 16,000 Knights of the Golden Circle, a pro-Confederate secret organization that was active and dangerous in all doubtful states in winning over to the southern cause those who feebly protested loyalty to the Union but who opposed war. Many of these Knights were prosperous and substantial citizens who, working under the guise of the respectability, exerted a profound influence.

Another class of men to be feared was a small but powerful group representing much wealth, a financial class which proverbially shuns war because on the expense which war involves; a class that always insists upon peace, even at the cost of compromised honor. These men with the influence which their money commanded, would inevitably espouse the side that seemed the most likely of speedy success; and in view of the early successes of the Confederate armies and the zealous preselecting of rebel sympathizers in their midst, they were a potential risk to loyal Californians.

The native Spanish or Mexican classes were also appealed to with the promise that land titled would be adjusted. Another group were squatters and trespassers who were occupying land to which they had no right. Added to all theses sources of danger was the attitude of the thousands of well-meaning people who, regardless of the rebel solicitations, were at first indifferent.

The crowning blow that hit the already perplexed populace was the split which took place within the Pacific Command at the declaration of war between the States. It is estimated that at least one-third of the officers of the Sixth Regiment, belonging to the Department of the Pacific, resigned their commission following Lincoln's inauguration, and practically all left with the avowed intention of taking positions in the Confederate army. These resignations crippled the service on the Pacific Coast until new officers could be sent to succeed them.

From the preceding information it is easy to see why the Knights had such an easy time infiltrating California. As has been seen before, at the outbreak of actual hostilities, members of the KGC were in the state. They came by way of the well-known routes in many guises--as miners, traders, settlers, and in various professions such as doctors, lawyers, and teachers. They usually traveled in small bands, rarely numbering over five or six in number. After reaching California, these groups divided into still smaller units, spread out, and set up organization headquarters throughout the state. The most active of the secessionist centers were in El Monte, San Bernardino, Los Angeles, San Luis Obispo, Mariposa, Stockton, Marysville, Sacramento, and San Francisco.

Having located themselves in the regions where they were to work, the Knights did whatever possible to hinder the efforts of the Federal Government to hold California. This they did in various ways, having to modify some of their methods that had been used in the East.

Those who moved into larger towns such as San Francisco found jobs of military importance or worked in the local government of the town. In an incredibly short period of time, these well-organized sympathizers completely dominated in San Francisco all the key positions in the arsenals, mint, navy yard, and local army post. The same process also took place in the city government, which in time became practically ineffectual in carrying out its duties.

The completeness of their control can be estimated from the following information: The primary object of the movement which numbered 100,000 men, was to take the Presidio, Mint, and Custom House at San Francisco, also the navy yard at Mare Island, and the arsenal at Benicia. Every government position at this time, with the exception of a few in the Mint, was held by a Southerner. With every condition favorable to them, nearly two thousand Southern sympathizers met in San Francisco, and from that number eight hundred picked men were delegated to capture everything in sight.

In smaller towns and rural areas the organization worked a little differently. In these agricultural or stock raising regions the Knights either bought up or ran off all worthy horseflesh. These animals were driven south over the best possible routes to Texas, where they were turned over to the Confederate Army. In any case, it was the plan to see that these animals were not to be available for the Union cause if California did stay with the Federal government.

Good examples of the infiltration into the local governments of two of these agricultural regions may be seen in the cases of Marysville and Tulare, where the KGC was so strongly entrenched that the membership rivaled that of many bigger cities in which the organization was active.

The organization that had developed in Marysville in a very short time controlled every office of authority in the town. In fact, the newspaper of the town Marysville "The Express" conducted a clearinghouse of all news and information for the KGC. The populace even had the audacity to fly palmetto flags on the day Lincoln was elected and to ask for a military commander from the South.

Another such group worked in Tulare, where, in due time, they too had control of the major offices in the town. They, like the KGC element in Marysville, gained control of the press and, after changing the name of the paper from the "Post" to the "Equal Rights Expositor," so aroused their adherents as to cause them to murder two volunteers from a nearby army camp.

While this last act led the militia to destroy the press and close the office of the "Expositor," no arrest were made nor would it have done any good to do so since the sheriff, judge, mayor, and city council members were all either members of the KGC or southern in their sympathies. Trouble in the form of open rebellion was beginning to pit American against American throughout the length and breadth of California.

A prayer printed on Thanksgiving Day, 1862, in the "Visalia Equal Rights Expositor" shows the degree to which brother was set against brother:

'O Lord, we thank thee for letting the rebels wallop us at the battle of Pittsbury Landing--for letting them smite us hip and thigh, even unto the destruction of 9,600 of our good loyal soldiers, and 463 of our officers; and for giving speed to their legs through the awful swamps of Chicahominy; and, O Lord, most especially do we thank thee for the licking they gave us at Bull Run the Second, and assisting our flight from that fatal field; and O Lord, never while we live will we forget Antietam, where we had 200,000 and they only 70,000--if they, O Lord, had happened to have had as many men as we, we'd a been a done gone in--and that friendly creek between us, the mountains that kept our boys from running.'

Usually the accounts put into print were not as subtle as the aforesaid article, but were rather loud and threatening in their narratives. However, no tale was mere talk. Throughout the state in the strong centers of secessionist activities, action became the password.

In the meantime, however, after some KGC groups had been so effective in Southern California, others were starting to create havoc in the Northern sections of the states by burning, plundering, and threatening loyal citizens and their property. Starting slowly at first, the secessionists stepped up their operations until by the year 1863. Alarming reports had become commonplace on the desk of Pacific Coast Commanding General's Office.

By the end of 1863 the army found it all but impossible to cope with the well-organized Knights and called on government detectives to assist it in its attempts to ascertain the strength and future plans of KGC. The detectives were responsible directly to provost the marshal's office. Many records contained in the "War of The Rebellion Records" attest as to the success of their job while working with the army. The provost marshal's office also did a commendable job in securing information on the organization's work. It was largely through the work of these two branches of the Federal Government that the Northern Section of California was, in a sense, checked from more destructive activities.

If the army felt it was having troubles in the Northern Section of the State, even while having the Knights under reasonable control, the Southern Part must be considered as running wild. This was especially the case with Los Angeles and San Bernardino counties.

A man by the name of Clarence E. Bennett, a brave loyalist from Southern California, was finally aroused to the point of sending a personal letter to Secretary of State, Seward in Washington D.C. in the hopes of getting some action against the Confederates and the KGC in California. Then shortly after having written Secretary Seward, Bennet managed to obtain a copy of the oath being given by the secessionists in Holcomb Valley and sent it on to General Sumner. It reads as follows:

PREAMBLE

'Whereas, a crisis has arrived in our political affairs which demands the closest scrutiny and strictest vigilance of every true patriot as an American citizen; and whereas, we view with regret and heartfelt sorrow the existence of a civil war now waged by one portion of the American people against another; and whereas, also we believe that this kind of war has been called into requisition by the present Executive of the United States without the assent of either branch of the American Congress in their legislative capacity; and believing this is an unjust, unholy, iniquitous, and unconstitutional war; therefore:

First: BE IT RESOLVED, that we, as a portion of the citizens of the United States, will support the Constitution as it now stands, together with the amendments thereunto appended, and that we will strictly adhere to the decisions of the Supreme Court of the United States made under said Constitution where a collision or difference of opinion has heretofore or may hereafter occur between citizens of one State and those of another or between States and the Federal Government, foreign citizens etc.

Second: BE IT FURTHER RESOLVED, that, in our opinion, the President has violated the most sacred palladium of American Liberty by the suspension of the writ of habeas corpus, and thus depriving an American citizen of having cause of his imprisonment inquired into by the proper tribunal.

Third: BE IT FURTHER RESOLVED, that we are in favor of sustaining the Southern States of the American Confederacy in all their constitutional rights; that we believe an unconstitutional war is now being waged against them to subject them to a taxation enormous and unequal and to deprive them in the end of their species of property called slaves.

Fourth: AND BE IT LASTLY RESOLVED, that we mutually pledge to each other our lives, our property, and our sacred honor to sustain our brethren of the Southern States in just defense of all their constitutional rights, whether invaded by the present Executive or by a foreign foe.

OBLIGATION

'I (persons name), here in the presence of these witnesses, before Almighty God, I promise and swear that I will not divulge or reveal any of the secrets of this institution to anyone except I know to be a brother (or to instruct candidates). I furthermore swear that I will obey the proper authorities when ordered to do so, and that I will assist a brother of this institution in his rights, individually or constitutionally, when required of me by him, if need be, with my life. All this I solemnly swear to obey, under the penalty of <u>being shot</u>: J. J. Willis, H.C. Minor, W.W.Y. Gall, William Kilgore, J.S. Banks, J.S. Seale, Charles Seale, John Hambleton, W. Foreman, Hamilton Foreman, Samuel Kelsey, James H. Wilson, R. Gaines, C. Bogert (candidate for senator).'

Charles E. Bennett went on to add: "The list of names I did not see. These were at the bottom of the obligation. I think there are many who are participators who have not signed, and I am assured there is a long list of those who have. The painter, one of the gang, is now employed making the flag. I copied this instrument of treason accurately. The headquarters of the traitors is in Holcomb Valley, and there is a strong organization. I think two companies of the U.S. troops better be sent here at once. One of the members says he thinks in two weeks fighting will commence in this town if there are no U.S. troops here. The rumored defeat of the Federal troops has strengthened them considerably. The oath is administrated while kneeling, with the left hand on the heart, the right hand upheld. Every Southerner has joined. Many, I think, join for plunder. There are additions every day. I think it best, as soon as the troops get here, to commence arresting and securing them. You see they have provided for that. As soon as one is arrested they are bound to release him. I will write soon if nothing happens to me."

> In haste, very respectably,
> CLARENCE E. BENNET

P.S. The grip: In taking hands, pass you little finger between his little finger and third finger. Pass words: I say: Are you on it? You reply, I am on it, at the same time carry your right hand to your right side to the pistol butt, as if to draw you revolver. Then I say, What's your name? You say, R-A-B-E. Use the letters to spell bear—bear flag.

There is ample evidence to sustain the claim that this organization was none other than the Knights of the Golden Circle. The fact that they were found in every part of the state explains the display of the Bear Flag early in the war at so many different points. It was virtually a bringing to life of the old ideas of a California Republic.

Election day especially proved hectic in San Bernardino and Capt. John W. Davidson, who was commanding, reported incident upon incident happening on that day. Following is a typical report:

'The day of the election at San Bernardino, I was directed by Major Ketchum to keep my squadron in hand near town to repress disorder, and not to leave until after the polls were closed...Meantime many persons gathered around my buggy (there were 200 or 300 people still near the polls), having sticks in their hands, and commenced shouting: "Hurrah for Jeff Davis! Hurrah for the Southern Confederacy!" Most of the persons had revolvers. One of them said that if the Union men felt themselves stronger there that day, they (the secessionists) could beat them robbing and burning any day. I rose in my buggy and called attention of the people to the fact that there were men in the midst who openly avowed themselves robbers and house burners, and gave comfort and heart to the enemies of the country by their shouts, and then turning through the crowd I drove over one man I believe, went down to my camp about 300 yards off, where the squadron was standing to horse, and brought up a platoon of dragoons, and riding into the crowd, stated that I would seize anyone who uttered the same cry named above.'

The results of the day's balloting caused a minor riot in Holcomb Valley, where the constable was forced in self-defense to kill an overzealous secessionist. An attempt was then made to lynch the peace officer but was frustrated.

The victory of Stanford was a shock to the Knights of the Golden Circle to be sure; but, if the Unionists believed the storm had been quelled, they were in for a surprise, for the Southerners were planning another attempt to usurp the power of the Government. This plan was already in operation, in a sense, in Southern California, especially in the mountain area of San Bernardino County. It was evidently to this operation, later to be known as the Hastings Scheme, that the "Alta California" was referring in its article of September 9, 1861. The article stated:

'I have pretty reliable information that at the San Bernardino mines, in an area of sixteen miles in diameter, there are not less than seven hundred men, mostly Secessionists, not more than two hundred and fifty of whom are even ostensibly engaged in mining. Most of these men have recently come there. I am confident that there are at this time upward of two thousand men in Los Angeles and San Bernardino Counties, completely organized and ready to rendezvous at such places as their leaders may direct. A large majority of this number are transient persons, and undoubtedly are controlled by a secret organization (KGC). Besides these, it is evident that a large number of able-bodied Californians have been seduced and drawn into the coils of the conspirators. What measures have been taken to provide arms and ammunition, or where they have obtained them, is involved in obscurity; but the stake for which the traitors are playing and the confidence in their countenances, warrant the conclusion they are nor deficient in either arms or finances.'

It seems thus that the Southern part of the State was the playground for the traitors of the Knights of the Golden Circle, even though they were without the support of the chief administration of the state and were supposedly under Union yoke. In fact, the secessionist were still in control. Loyal Unionists still were held in contempt and often had to fear for their lives. The inability of the Union Army to deal with these disloyal elements caused no small amount of consternation among the patriotic people in this section of the state.

Protest after protest was sent to the Commanding General of the Pacific Coast, soliciting his aid. The army, however, had more than they could do already and to divert more men and weapons to these secessionists' strongholds was impossible.

The army reports and newspaper editions of 1861-1863 bear undeniable testimony to the increasing frequency with which rebels insulted or destroyed property belonging to the Federal Government without reprisals of any kind. To be sure, the troops were still in these dissatisfied areas, but to little or no effect. Quantrell-type raids to acquire horses were on the increase and nearly every rancher in the Southland suffered.

By 1863 the Federal Government in California, even with its shortage of troops, was compelled to do something or admit that it was ineffectual against the KGC organization. To carry out its intelligence in the Southern section of the State, the Government once again found it necessary to use Government detectives.

Once again, these men did a remarkable job for the service. Report after report proved their worth, however, even they had their moments of doubt and wonder. This was especially true when they uncovered a grandiose plan conceived by one Lansford W. Hastings. Hastings' plan, if implemented and brought to bear fruit, would have overthrown the Federal government in Arizona and New Mexico and claimed these in the name of the Confederacy. To implement his plans, Hastings would gather the men congregating in the mountains and around San Bernardino and march south through Arizona and seize Fort Yuma which was known as the "California Bastille." No other personage than Jeff Davis and his Generals were considering the plausibility of such a plan and were in close contact with Hastings.

(Authors Note: A short reference to the Hastings Plan was mentioned in an American History book for high school seniors that I used, but no mention was ever made of the KGC.)

The southerners were not as convinced of the scheme though as Hastings was, and refused financial aid. However, if they had seen fit to aid this plan, perhaps the history of the Pacific coast and the rest of the war might be read differently now.

The failure of aid coming via the South stopped the scheme's being put into action; but large numbers of men still lingered in these areas until shortly after Lincoln's assassination, when they finally spread throughout the state once again.

In conclusion, one may state positively that the Knights of the Golden Circle organization was an instrument of war and conquest used and developed by the South to further Southern expansion, from the days when, as "The Lone Star," it had helped to foment the war with Mexico in Texas. It was bent on Southern expansion into Mexico and Central American States until halted by the outbreak of the Civil War, at which time it was sent north to accomplish its purpose.

In general, its goals were to hinder the Northern states in anyway possible. This was done in various ways, as has been seen. Its major objective, as far as California was concerned, was to swing the State to the Southern side of the conflict and, if this was not possible, to see that the state did as little as possible to aid the Federal Government.

CONCLUSION

The ending of the war saw the end of the Knights of the Golden Circle as an active group in California. Many of the members returned to the South while others remained and settled down to become part of the population. The more lawless element headed south into Mexico, plundering the state as they went. Such groups brought shame and embarrassment to those of Southern extraction in California.

Many members of the KGC, one can safely assume, became members of the Ku Klux Klan when it was instituted in the South--in fact, there seems to be great similarity in the two rituals of the past and present organizations.

NOTE: The preceding 12 pages were taken directly from the San Bernardino County Museum Association Quarterly, Volume XV, No. 4 Summer, 1968; and is reprinted here (as written) for the purpose of enlightening the reader to the fact that this little-known but very large and extremely powerful organization, did exist; and to show how well organized, determined, and dedicated they were to carry out the Confederate cause.

Though the preceding material does not make any references to the vast amount of money and riches they later accumulated then buried at many locations around the country for the purpose of restarting the Civil War again, it's because that part happened after most of this material had been written. An organization such as this with such determined and grandioso plans would certainly not be expected to suddenly give up and cease-and-desist just because an armistice had been signed to halt hostilities, but would be expected to keep on trying. And this they certainly did by going underground with secret meetings to carry on what they had so determinably been trying to do for years. They needed money and materials to accomplish that…thus the reason for the treasures they hid, as we will see later in this book.

BIBLIOGRAPHY

Pitman, Benn, editor. "Trials for Treason at Indianapolis." Official Report of the Judge Advocate General on the Order of American Knights, or Sons of Liberty, A Western Conspiracy In Aid of the Southern Rebellion. Moore, Wilstarch, and Baldwin, 1865.

Pomfrey, J.W. "True disclosure and Exposition of the Knights of the Golden Circle." Author, 1861. Obtained from National Archives, Washington, D.C., on microfilm.

Stidger, F.G. "Treason History of the Order of the Sons of Liberty." Published by Author, (Leonard B. Waitman) 1903.

Winslow, Ayer. "The Great Treason Plot in the Northwest During the War." Chicago: U.S. Publishing Company, 1895.

PUBLIC DOCUMENTS

Microfilm: "Diary of Samuel J. Pealer, 1362-64. National Archives, Washington D.C.

Microfilm: "History of Camp Cady," 1865-1871. National Archives, Washington D.C.

Microfilm: KGC, George W. Bickley's Address to The people of Raleigh, North Carolina, 1860. Henry E. Huntington Library, San Marino, California.

Union Congressional Committee, "The Copperhead Conspiracy in the North West." Library of Congress, Washington D.C., 1864.

"War of the Rebellion," Official Records of the Union and Confederate Armies." Series One, Vol. One L, Part II, Correspondence, etc. Operations on—the Pacific Coast July 1, 1862—June 30, 1865 (Serial No. 106) Washington: Government Press, 1897.

ARTICLES

Dustin, Charles Mial. "The Knights of the Golden Circle; the story of the Pacific Coast Secessionist," Pacific Monthly. Vol. 26, Nov. 1911.

Leland, Charles G. "Sketch," in Continental Monthly. Vol. 1, 1862.

Chapter Two

Knights of The Golden Circle— Treason History, 1864

During my research for this publication, the most complete and detailed works that I found was a book entitled: *Knights of the Golden Circle-- Treason History, Sons of Liberty, 1864,* with a subheading that read as follows:

"Treason History of the Order of Sons of Liberty, Formerly Circle of Honor, Succeeded by Knights of the Golden Circle. Afterward, Order of American Knights. The Most Gigantic Treasonable Conspiracy the World Has Ever Known, by Felix G. Stidger."

Stidger was born in Kentucky in 1836, and became a United States Government Secret Service Agent who was assigned to infiltrate the Knights of the Golden Circle for the purpose of gathering evidence for the Government to bring charges of sedition against various members and leaders of the group. Stidger was very successful in penetrating the organization and eventually became a member of high standing as: The Grand Secretary of State, Order of Sons of Liberty, State of Kentucky in 1864.

The information that Stidger gathered that he later put into book form in 1903 was the sole reliance of the United States Government for detailed information of the work of these conspirators and the only man the government could put upon the witness stand at their trial for treason for the personal identification of the conspirators, including one of their great leaders, Harrison H. Dodd who was sentenced to be hanged to death.

The book has 275 pages of information never printed before for the public. I have extracted some pages from some of the sections that give great insight into their manner of thinking and their ambitions that include: "The Unwritten Secret Work of the Order of Sons of Liberty," which includes their secret grips, signs, passwords, etc.; also an appendix that gives an explanation of the initial letters used in the rituals; then a few pages of the secret" Rituals of the Order of Sons of Liberty," starting with the Neophyte or Vestibul Degree, which I found to be most revealing. This rare bit of secret information is reproduced here for the first time in the following pages:

Unwritten Secret Work
OF THE
Order of Sons of Liberty.

I have seen several publications of these Rituals of the Knights of the Golden Circle, Order of American Knights, and Order of Sons of Liberty, but have never seen one that could be deciphered as to what Degree of the Order it could be properly applied. The original pamphlets could not be so applied—if the covers were destroyed,—by anyone unfamiliar with the Order, and it is only from my personal knowledge and familiarity in the use of the original pamphlets that I am able to correctly designate them.

The Ritual of the Knights of the Golden Circle was that used in the Neophyte or Vestibule, Degree of the Order of Sons of Liberty. Members of this Degree were *never* given an account of the workings or intentions of the Order. If, after making themselves sufficiently familiar with this Degree, they were found worthy to be trusted further with the secrets of the Order they were then admitted to the First Temple Degree of the Order, and further instructed in the designs and intentions of the Order, but then not fully admitted to the secrets until they had fully shown themselves as worthy to the full confidence of the Order, when they were admitted into the Second and Third Temple Degrees of the Order and fully instructed in its revolutionary designs and intentions. It was a case sometimes that a member of the lower degrees would be given some information of the higher degrees before being admitted into the higher degrees, but this was always given by, and at the risk of the higher degree member who gave the information.

The members of the Neophyte or Vestibule Degree were as much bound to the obedience of the Officers of the Order as those of the higher or Temple Degrees, but there was not the trust reposed in them as in the members of the higher degrees of the Order, and not as much trust reposed in the members of the First Temple Degree as in those of the Second and Third Temple Degrees.

GRIPS, SIGNS, PASSWORDS, ETC.

THESE HAVE NEVER BEFORE BEEN PUBLISHED.

The Order was so arranged, that one taking the Neophyte or Vestibule Degree knew nothing of the real intentions of the Order further than what the instructions in that degree alone gave him, and in large towns and cities the members of that degree would meet as general political clubs. They would be bound by the obligation of the Order of Sons of Liberty, but knew nothing further of the organization than that Degree. (For the obligation, declaration of principles, etc., see "Ritual of the Order of Sons of Liberty" in this Appendix.)

There are, in the unwritten work, signs, grips, colloquies and pass-words, used in the recognition and testing of members, as follows: A member of the Neophyte Degree on meeting a stranger whom he supposes to be a member of the Order would test him in the signs of the degree thus; Standing erect on both feet, placing the heel of the right foot in the hollow of the left, with the right hand under the left arm, bringing the left hand under the right arm, thus folding the arms, and placing the four fingers of the left hand over the right arm; the stranger, or person addressed, if a member of the Order, will take the same position. That is as far as you go in public. You both then retire to some place where you will not be observed, and continue the test. You advance your right foot, and he will advance his right foot to meet yours, the feet partly passing each-other; the two then take an ordinary grip with the right hands, at the same time placing the left hand on the right breast. If you find him incorrect you stop. If you find him correct you proceed with the following colloquy, which is given in alternate syllables by each of you; first, the pass-word of the Order for that Degree, which is "Calhoun," syllableized and spelled backwards, thus; I would begin "nu," he reply "oh," I continue "laC," he would then say "S," I would answer "L," when he would say, "Give me liberty," and I would reply, "or give me death;" then you give one shake of the hand. In this Neophyte Degree there is also a signal of distress. This is given by placing the left hand on the right breast and raising the right hand and arm to full height one time, if it is in day-time; if at night, when that could not be seen, you give the night signal of distress by calling out the word oak-oun three times, thus; oak-oun, oak-oun, oak-oun; you wait a moment, and if you receive no reply or assistance you call again, oak-oun, three times as before, and continue this signal until you obtain assistance. The members of this degree were instructed that it was the duty of each member of the Order on seeing or hearing the signal of distress to immediately respond to the call and assist the member in distress. "Oak" is the tree of the acorn, which is the symbolical emblem of the Order, and "oun" is the last syllable of the pass-word, as it is usually pronounced. If the person was not considered worthy to take any further degrees he was not advanced further, and never knew anything officially of the further organization of the Order.

In the First Temple Degree of the Order the sign of recognition is by placing the feet and arms the same as in the Neophyte Degree, except, that in place of four fingers over the right arm, the first two fingers are so placed, and they are separated; this position of the fingers is taught to have reference to State,s rights and State sovereignty, If a member gives that sign it is the duty of another seeing it to advance and recognize him. In taking the grip each one moves his first finger upon the wrist of the other, taking the ordinary grip with the other three fingers, running the thumbs as nearly straight as possible. This grip is taught to be as near the shape of the acorn—the universal emblem of the Order—as can be made with the hand, and representing strength, growth, and durability; the left hand to be placed on the breast as before. The colloquy is repeated thus: "If I go to the East"—"I will go to the West"—"Let there be no strife"—"between mine and thine"—"for we"—"be brethren." "O"—"S"—"L"—"Resistance to tyrants"—"is obedience to God." (The colloquies are pronounced alternately, as in the Neophyte Degree.) Great care is taken to say "be brethren," the word "be" being a test of membership. The part of this colloquy after the initials "O. S. L.," is said to have been added by Vallandigham, when the work of the Order was sent to him for revision after the committee at New York had revised the ritual in February, 1864. In this Degree members were instructed in the manner of entering a temple. The pass-word of this Degree was changed monthly in each County Temple, which adopted its own pass-word. Those initiated into this Degree were welcomed as full members of the Order of Sons of Liberty, except they were not permitted to represent the Temple in the Grand Council of the State until they had taken the Second and Third Temple Degrees.

The Second Temple Degree; The feet are placed and advanced as before; the hands are crossed on the abdomen, the right hand on the outside, to represent the belt of Orion; the thumbs pointing upwards, to represent the point of the Star Arcturus. The colloquy is repeated thus: "What"—"a Star"—"Arc"—"turus,"—"What of the night"—"morning cometh,"—"will ye inquire"—"inquire ye,"—"return,"—"come." This colloquy is taken mostly from the 11th and 12th verses of the 21st Chapter of Isaiah. The pass-word of this Degree is "Orion," pronounced as a test by giving the long sound to "i" the second syllable. The grip of this Degree is the ordinary grip, with the thumbs of the joined hands pointing upwards, representing the point of the Star Arcturus. Members were instructed that a five-pointed star of any metal could be used as an emblem of this Degree.

The Third Temple Degree; The feet are placed and

advanced as before; the arms are crossed on the breast, with the fingers pointing to the shoulders, the right arm on the outside. This sign is said to represent the Southern Cross as seen in the Heavens South of the Equator. The colloquy is given thus: "Whence"—"Seir,"—"How"—"By the ford,"—"Name it"—"Jaback,"—"Thy password"—"Washington"—"Bayard." The distinct pronunciation of the last syllable, "yard," being a test of membership. "Washington" is the pass-word of the Degree. The grip is given by locking the thumbs crosswise, the palms of the hands held downwards, and the hands held horizontal. It is a grip of the thumbs only. If, as a stranger, you wish to visit any lodge, you give three knocks on the door; when the wicket is raised you give your name, residence, rank, and the Temple to which you belong. If you are known by any member present you are admitted; if you are not known a committee is sent out to examine you. They test you, and if they find you are perfect in every particular they report to the lodge, and you are admitted; if you fail in any respect they know you no more.

The Grand Council Degree; The feet are placed and advanced the same as in the Neophyte and Temple Degrees; the right arm is placed as in the Third Temple Degree, the left hand being placed under the right elbow; you then take the ordinary grip with the right hands, and with the left hand, each taking hold of the right elbow of the other, and give one shake of the hands; then take the exact position of folding the arms as in the Neophyte Degree; then each turn one-fourth around to the right, facing in opposite directions, and with the arms still folded, the colloquy is given thus: "Whence"—"America"—"North"—"South." "America" is the pass-word of the Grand Council Degree.

There is reference in the Ritual to a passage of Scripture given in the initiation as part of the charge, Isaiah LIX:14-19. This passage, as well as the "Invocations," is said to have been added to the ritual by Vallandigham.

APPENDIX.

EXPLANATION

OF THE

INITIAL LETTERS USED IN THE RITUALS.

O. A. K.

W. O. C. Warden of Outer Court.
K. L. Knight Lecturer.
K. C. Knight Conductor.
N. Neophyte.
A. B. Ancient Brother.
K. G. N. Knight Guardian North.
K. G. S. Knight Guardian South.
G. S. Grand Seignior.
The above belongs to the First Degree of the Order of American Knights.
E. K. C. W. Excellent Knight Commander West.

E. K. Excellent Knight.
E. K. G. C. Excellent Knight Grand Commander.
O. A. K. Order of American Knights.
The above belongs to the Second Degree of the Order of American Knights.
M. E. K. Most Excellent Knight.
M. E. D. O. A. K. Most Excellent Degree of the O. A. K.
M. E. G. C. Most Excellent Grand Commander.

O. S. L.

NEOPHYTE OR VESTIBULE LESSON.

V. Vestibule.
W. O. C. Warden Outer Court.
L. V. Lecturer of the Vestibule.
O. C. Outer Court.
T. Temple.

FIRST DEGREE.

O. S. L. Order of Sons of Liberty.
C. T. Conductor of the Temple.
W. Warden.
A. B. Ancient Brother (second officer of First Degree.)
A. S. L. A Son of Liberty.
O. Order.
F. G. N. Fellow Guardian North.
F. G. S. Fellow Guardian South.
G. S. Grand Seignior (first officer of First Degree.)
F. O. S. L. Fellow in the Order of Sons of Liberty.

SECOND DEGREE, OR FIRST CONCLAVE DEGREE.

K. O. S. L. Knight Order of Sons of Liberty.
K. C. Knight Conductor.
K. C. W. Knight Commander West, (second officer.)
I. T. Inner Temple.
C. C. Commander Conclave.
T. D. Temple Degree.

G. C. Grand Council.
S. C. Supreme Council.
K. C. C. Knight Commander of Conclave.
I. T. of O. Inner Temple of the Order.

THIRD DEGREE, OR SECOND CONCLAVE DEGREE.

M. E. K. O. S. L. Most Excellent Knight Order of Sons of Liberty.
M. E. K. C. W. Most Excellent Knight Commander West.
K. C. Knight Conductor.
M. E. K's. Most Excellent Knights.
M. E. K. O. S. L. Most Excellent Knights Order of Sons of Liberty.
M. E. G. C. Most Excellent Grand Commander.
I—t T. Innermost Temple.
C. Conclave.
G. C. S. Grand Council of the State.
S. C. O. S. L. Supreme Council Order of Sons of Liberty.
K. C. C. Knight Commander of Conclave.

STATE GRAND COUNCIL.

G. C. Grand Council, or Grand Commander.
Dep. G. C. Deputy Grand Commander.
G. C. S. S. C. Grand Counselor S. Supreme Council.
S. G. C. Supreme Grand Council.

RITUALS

OF THE

Order of Sons of Liberty,

NEOPHYTE OR VESTIBULE DEGREE.

W. O. C. Gives * * * (Three knocks.)

K. L. Who cometh? Who cometh? Who cometh?

W. O. C. A man! We found him in the hands of the sons of despotism, bound in chains, and well nigh crushed to death beneath the iron heel of the oppressor. We have brought him hither, and would fain clothe him in the white robes of Virtue, and place his feet in the straight and narrow path which leads to Truth and Wisdom.

K. L., Brothers! The purpose ye have declared touching this stranger is most worthy; let him advance to our altar by the regular steps; instruct him in our chosen, solemn attitude, and let him give testimony of that which is in him.

K. L. DIVINE ESSENCE! GOD OF OUR FATHERS, whose inspiration moved them to mighty deeds of valor in the cause of Eternal Truth, Justice and Human Rights. We, their sons, would fain recognize the same presence and inspiration in this V. of the T., consecrated to the principles which they inculcated by precept and by example, and defended with their lives and their sacred honor. With the DIVINE PRESENCE let holiest memories come, like incense to our souls, and exalt them with emotions worthy of the ceremonies of the Supreme occasion. *Amen!*

Man! Thou art now in the V., and, if found worthy, will hence be ushered into the consecrated T., where Truth dwells amid her votaries; let thy soul be duly conscious of her presence, and go forth in exalted desire for her divine influence. Within those sacred precincts, rev-

Refer to the appendix on the preceding page for the initials used here.

erence toward the Supreme Being, Patriotism, Love, Charity and good fellowship are inculcated and cherished. Infidelity to God or our country, nor hatred, nor malice, nor uncharitableness, nor their kindred vices, must enter there. "Love one another," is the *hail* of the order into whose inner circle thou wouldst fain be inducted. Direct thy thoughts within, at this supreme moment, and declare, as thou wouldst answer to a good conscience, is thy soul pure and fitted for the indwelling of Truth?

Answer, "yes," or "no."

Is thy heart quickened with genial emotions toward thy fellow man? Answer, "yes," or "no."

It is well. If thou hast not answered truly, in obedience to the promptings of thy holier nature, so shalt thou be judged in the last day, when the secrets of thy heart shall be revealed, and the actions and purposes of thy life on earth shall return to thy soul their fruits of bitterness or joy eternal. I charge thee, if thou art impelled hitherward by curiosity; if thou cherish other purposes, in this regard, than the highest and the holiest which thy heart can conceive, it were better for thee that thy feet had never passed the threshold of our outer court. Our faithful and beloved brothers, who have conducted thee hither into this presence, are thy sponsors. A fearful responsibility is upon them! If thou should falsify their assurances to us, betray us, betray their trust, or stain thy manhood by unworthy actions, it will be their painful duty to publish thy shame, so that thou art expelled, and ever after excluded from the society of honorable men.

Brothers, explain your obligations as sponsors for the candidate.

OBLIGATION OF THE SPONSORS.

"We do solemnly promise and undertake, amidst the inspiring associations of our sacred V., that the stranger whom we have introduced into this presence, shall in all things prove himself a true man. That from his daily walk and conversation with his fellows, we guarantee his worthiness to be inducted into the sublime mysteries of our beloved order. We do further promise and undertake for him, that he shall faithfully keep secret whatsoever shall transpire in this presence. We do further promise, that if he shall be found worthy thereto, and shall be advanced to the inner T. of our order, that he shall reveal nothing which shall therein be made known to him to be preserved an inviolate secret. We do further promise that, in case he shall betray the confidence which he has inspired in us, we will hold it our bounden duty to see that he is expelled from the association of all honorable men. This we do promise with the approbation of the DIVINE SPIRIT. Amen!

Hast thou heard and considered the words, promises and obligations of thy sponsors? Answer, "Aye."

Wilt thou, imploring aid from the DIVINITY within thee, perform unto the end that which they have promised in thy behalf? Answer, "I will."

It is well! God help thee unto the end!

It is now my duty to explain the principles which our order inculcates, holding them for sublime and eternal truths, and which we, as an organized fraternity, and as individuals, aim to illustrate in our lives and conversations, as well in our intercourse with men as in our sacred conclave. Listen to the words of wisdom, and let them sink deep into thy heart.

This old rare book was discovered by Stanley Vickery a few years ago, then acquired by Don Marler of Dogwood Press who has reprinted the book. It can be ordered from him at: HC Box 345, Hemphill, Texas, 75948. Phone (409) 579-2184 for $24.00 plus shipping and handling. Web site is demsmm@inu.net

Chapter Three

Jesse James III. The Man Who Said He Knew Where The Knights Buried Their Treasures.

The purpose of this book in the preceding chapters was to present enough historical documents to show the reader that the Knights of The Golden Circle did exist and to demonstrate how large, extensive and powerful they really were--almost equal to the two major political parties at the time, especially since they crossed not only party lines, but even into the military forces, and they all had feverant sympathies with the Confederate cause.

Just how large were they? They certainly numbered up into the hundreds of thousands, and the measure of their strength is shown by just how close they came to accomplishing all other goals; and some they certainly did, such as getting Texas into the Union and also as a Southern slave State.

Perhaps though, some may be a bit skeptical about this information and what has been documented in the past, but so was I at first when I began to hear reports about their organization and how vast and powerful it really was; especially since nothing had ever been mentioned about them in any of the history books that I had read while going to school.

However, as I became more and more involved in searching for lost mines and buried treasures and also as a major writer on these subjects, I began to learn of their organization and the huge treasures and military equipment they amassed (with the serious and full intent to restart the Civil War) it attracted my attention. All during this time, I was working full time as an aeronautical engineer with various aerospace companies in Los Angeles and writing for the treasure publications in my spare time.

Then one day in 1974, I saw a full-page feature story in one of the major Los Angeles newspapers about the Knights of the Golden Circle and the hundreds of millions of dollars worth of treasure they had left behind. This was the first time that story had appeared in the media. The next day I called the paper and spoke to the reporter. He was Del Schrader, a veteran newspaper reporter for many years. We soon had lunch together and my life was never the same again. That newspaper story is shown here in its entirety at the end of this chapter.

JESSIE JAMES III. THE GREAT GRANDSON OF JESSE JAMES

Del had been in contact with a man who lived in Banning. California, located a few miles east of Los Angeles, and it was from him that Del had gained the information. The man said that his name was Jesse James III, the great-grandson of the famous outlaw from Missouri, Jesse James, and that Jesse had not been killed by Bob Ford as was generally believed. However, I learned later that his real name might have been Frank Hawks (or maybe Howks) who had been living in Waco, Texas before coming to California. Also he had lived in New Mexico where he was involved in searching for a lost Jesse James treasure that apparently resulted in a major recover, which ended up in a lawsuit over the ownership. (See the newspaper story regarding that event also at the end of this chapter.)

WAS JESSE JAMES STILL ALIVE IN OKLAHOMA IN 1948?

Now, this gentleman was most interesting as I found out later. At first, I went along with whom he said he was, since many people were still believing that Bob Ford did not kill Jesse James in 1882, and it was all a clever fake just to convince the law that Jesse was dead and to close the case on him. This belief was fostered by a number of things. One of them was an amazing story that broke through the newspapers in 1948 that showed a photograph with a story of a man living in Lawton, Oklahoma that claimed he was 104 years old and was the real life Jesse Woodson James. He told many stories that seemed to be convincing and even showed the scars from many bullet holes that seemed to match those from the real Jesse James, except the one in the back of his head where he was presumably shot to death. He also had rope burns around his neck and some knife wounds. He said that he had been living under a number of assumed names, including, Bob Dalton, a cousin of Jesse James. He also seemed to convince some people who were still alive and had known the real Jesse James, that he was indeed not an impostor. Apparently, no one has proven convincingly that he was not the real Jesse James, and the argument goes on even to this day. (See the newspaper story at end of this chapter.)

However, I personally have gradually come to the conclusion that he was not alive, and that the real Jesse James was shot to death by his friend Bob Ford in 1882. But I must admit that I'm not absolutely positive. According to a television program that I saw several years ago, some forensic scientist were hired in 1995 to exhume the body that was buried in the grave that was marked as that of Jesse Woodson James. During the procedure, several peculiar things came to light. One of them was that the body had been buried face downward. Why? That was a very odd thing especially in those days of doing things in a customary manner. Of course, the casket had been made of wood and was badly deteriorated, as was the body also. The investigators also said they recovered a bullet that had been fired by a revolver in the area of the head and the skull was badly shattered from the bullet, but the records claim that the bullet passed through his head and embedded itself in the wall. In fact, I have an old photograph of that wall in one of my books on Western History that shows where souvenir hunters dug into the wall to recover it. Therefore, the bullet should not have been buried with him. So, something does not add up here.

The investigators claimed that enough DNA was recovered to compare with some supposedly living relatives in Oklahoma, and the results apparently showed that the relatives in Oklahoma shared the same DNA. However, press reports on the incident claimed that the report on the DNA was untrue. It seems to be logical that if some one is hired to prove a point, it will usually happen.

But regardless of what they think the DNA test revealed, why was the body in the grave buried face downward. Was it to hide the possibility that it was someone else and not Jesse James? If so, wasn't it a clever way to hide the real identity of the corpse? It could have been anybody. Also, why was a bullet found with the body that should not have been there according to the records?

WHO WAS REALLY BURIED IN JESSE JAMES'S GRAVE?

It has been written up in many books and articles that the real corpse was a man named Charlie Bigelow who had been killed and buried instead of the real Jesse James. So, if there's no more proof than a deteriorated body that had been shot in the back of the head and buried face-down under a Jesse James tombstone, possibly it is not the body of Jesse James, but the result of a very clever plot. Jesse James was a clever man and there is no doubt that such a plot was not beyond him. One of his favorite tricks was to have the shoes of his horse put on backwards to fool any posse trying to follow his trail.

I'm sure that the debate will go on long into the future as to whether the real Jesse James was killed in 1882, or not, and whether or not he went on to be a leading member of the Knights of the Golden Circle and robbed for the purpose of donating money to them to support their plans of restarting the Civil War. It's not beyond a reasonable doubt. He was known to be anti-union and had at one time, rode with the famous southern raider, Quantrill. Also, it seems to be a fact that of all the banks he robbed and all of the money he got, very little, if any has ever been recovered, and there are no mentions of Jesse ever having or spending a lot of money. So possibly, he did contribute it to the KGC treasury.

In fact, let's look at a simple scenario that could very easily be true. The Governor of Missouri had offered a $25,000 reward for Jesse James...dead or alive! The "dead" part was the key to making the scenario work. With a price like that on his life, Jesse knew that sooner or later someone, friend, foe or even a relative, would take advantage of the offer. After all, $25,000 was a huge amount in those days. This of course, made Jesse nervous and he knew that his days under those circumstances would be numbered, even though he was living secretly under the assumed name of Mr. Howard. It should not have been hard to figure out a plan that would satisfy everybody involved, plus gaining the reward money. Why not formulate a plan whereby with the help of his friend, Bob Ford, they would use somebody else's body, like somebody they didn't like, or someone they just found convenient. Or maybe the victim was really Charlie Bigelow, as has been claimed.

THE PLOT

First, they had to make up a story that when Bob Ford and his brother came to visit Jesse, he shot Jesse in the back of the head when Jesse "Uncustomary removed his gun and gun belt and placed them on the bed," (as reported in one of the newspapers), turned his back, climbed up on a chair, and reached up to straighten a crooked picture on the wall.

I have to admit that I have always thought the story was a bit strange and maybe a bit contrived--and always passed it off as just part of the reported story that may or may not have been accurate. It was well known that Jesse wore his guns nearly all of the time--even while at home since he never trusted anybody, especially two men together; and he had always said that he would never be taken alive. But I never really saw any particular significance to the story, until now.

So, with a plan worked out ahead of time, someone that appeared similar to Jesse was shot in the back of the head, put in the casket, and buried with a headstone that identified him as Jesse Woodson James. Of course, there had to be some cooperation from his friends and family to make it work.

But, what about the photograph of the body of Jesse James in the casket before he was buried? Well, that's not hard to figure out. Jesse could have been lying there alive and not dead--though possibly he played dead long enough to fool the photographer while taking the picture. After all, precautions had to be taken. Also, if you take a good look at the photograph, there is no evidence of any damage to the front of the head. It looks intact, although the reports claim that the bullet passed through his head and embedded itself in the wall.

But wait--there is more! That photograph shows Jesse lying face up, but when the body was exhumed in 1993, it was lying face down. How come? Well, probably after the photograph was taken of Jesse lying face up, the other person was buried face down with the excuse from the family that they didn't want to show the disfigured front of the head. Yes, of course! That all fits perfectly and is the only thing that makes sense out of the situation. And if that was the case, then the stories about Jesse James living on for years under assumed names could be true.

JESSE JAMES III...OR WAS HE FRANK HAWKS?

So, who was this man that claimed he was Jesse James III, the one that I had met? Was he faking, or was he really a great grandson of Jesse James? If he was faking, then why was he doing that? Well, it's mostly speculation on my part, but I think it was partly to help support his living since he was not employed anywhere. Or maybe because he enjoyed the attention and the intrigue of acting out the life of a famous historical personality, and as a treasure hunter. One thing that I can positively say about him was that he was exceptionally brilliant and had a remarkable memory of many things that I knew to be true. His knowledge on the subject a treasure was vast. Del Schrader and I both agreed that if the had chosen to apply his ability to the business world, legally and straight, he would have been very successful. But maybe he would have found that too boring.

TREASURES MAPS

But just because he could be lying about his identity, that did not mean that he was lying about what he said regarding the treasure of the Knights of the Golden Circle. I'm convinced that he had researched extensively and had accumulated much accurate information on the subject matter. He passed on some of his maps to me that he had been working on so that we could make plans to go look for them. Del Schrader did go to one of the sites in Montana, but could not get on the property since it had a strong fence around it and was heavily posted with many no trespassing signs.

The first weekend after Dell wrote his story on the Knights of the Golden Circle, we drove to Banning, California, located only a few miles east of Los Angeles. It was a most fascinating day. Jesse James III entertained us both with numerous stories and information on the treasures of Knights of the Golden Circle and the men who had (and some who still were) involved with it. Then he showed us photos and maps. I was amazed.

Over the next few months, I received numerous letters from him, all on the subject of the Knights, their treasures, and about Jesse James who he claimed was his great grandfather. Later, Del and I made a few more trips to visit with him.

One of the most intriguing treasures that he kept talking about was one located at the old Pigeon Ranch at Glorieta Pass in New Mexico which had been the location of the largest Civil War Battle west of the Mississippi River. This happened in March, 1862. He claimed, convincingly, that during the battle, Jesse James was there as a scout and a spy for the Confederates and the Knights the Golden Circle, and that he and some companions held up the paymaster with the payroll for the Union Army and buried it there. Later, it became a treasure of the Knights of the Golden Circle.

It sounded very interesting. But why was he showing this valuable information to us? The answer was not hard to figure out. He knew that I was an experienced treasure hunter and since I had some of the best metal detecting equipment available, he would like someone like me to form a partnership with to go look for the treasure.

As our plans progressed, he did not ask for money (which is normally the case) so he was not just selling the information as I've had experience with so many times before. However, Del and I did go together and pay $30 each for a dentist to work on his bad teeth.

At first, the plans were for all three of us to go on the trip. We each were to receive one-third of the treasure. However, he began to suffer from the effects of bad teeth and decided not to go, but he provided us with the necessary information to go on. Then, Del thought that he and I should have a little backup, so he invited a friend, John McFarland, who had once been a star football player for USC, to join us. Now, the division was to be one-quarter each. John was about 65 years old, but still in pretty good shape. Del had become a little nervous since he had heard Jesse James III mention that some of the sites were booby-trapped with explosives, and some had armed sentinels still watching over them--or both. This coincided with some rumors that I had already heard from other sources.

(Above) This photo shows the author, on the left, during his first meeting in 1973 with the man who said he was Jesse James III, the great-grandson of Jesse James, at his home in Banning, California.

(Right) Photo showing the Los Angeles Herald Examiner reporter, Del Schrader, with Jesse James III.

REWARDS

$500 REWARD

For the Arrest and Conviction of

JESSE JAMES

St. Louis Midland Railroad

$25,000 REWARD JESSE JAMES DEAD OR ALIVE

$15,000 REWARD FOR FRANK JAMES

$5000 Reward for any Known Member of the James Band

SIGNED:
ST. LOUIS MIDLAND RAILROAD

Jesse James was the most wanted man in America with a record reward out for him... dead or alive. These posters, years apart, tell their own story about the effectiveness of rewards.

This is a photograph of Jesse James supposedly taken after he was shot to death through the head by Bob Ford. When the body in Jesse James' grave was exhumed in the 1990's for the purpose of obtaining DNA, they found the skull badly shattered and that the body was buried upside down. But this photograph shows no sign of a badly shattered skull nor where the bullet passed out through his forehead as the reports said. Could this have been a posed photograph with Jesse still alive (facing upwards) and the body of another man buried instead? Has the world been deceived all these years?

In 1950, this 102-year-old man showed up at Fort Sill, Oklahoma, claiming that he was the real Jesse James. He said he'd been living under the assumed name of J. Frank Dalton and other aliases for 70 years, and that Bob Ford had killed Charles Bigelow, a member of the James gang, as a scheme to collect the award, and so that Jesse could escape from the law. When this man died in 1951, the official autopsy report showed that he had all of the physical characteristics of Jesse, including the color of his eyes. The report also showed that he had led a very rugged and dangerous life since he had many bullet wounds, evidence of rope burns around his neck, powder burns across his chin, one finger tip chewed off, plus other scars and injuries. He tried to get his name restored, but the judge refused saying that he had no authority to "restore" his name.

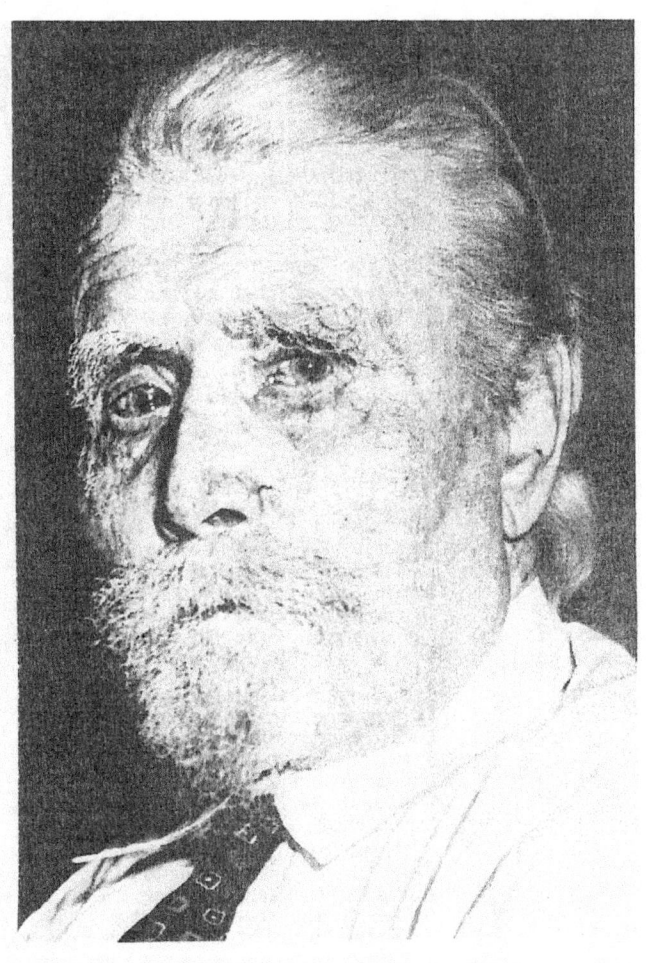

This photo shows the old man who said he was the real Jesse James (on the right) with the famous, early-day Oklahoma train robber, Al Jennings, who said, "Boys, there isn't a bit of doubt on earth. It's him. It's Jesse James." But Al wasn't the only one who said the man was Jesse James. A number of other people who had actually known Jesse came forward, and they all said that he really was Jesse James. Could they all have been wrong?

Man Who Insists He's Jesse James Says He Has $2,000,000 Buried Near Fort Sill

NEW YORK, Jan. 10 —(UP)— Jesse James, that is the latest man to claims he's the notorious outlaws, said Wednesday he has $2,000,000 in loot buried near Fort Sill, Okla.

He also said in passing that there never was a James gang.

The latest Jesse said he has been known since 1882 as J. Frank Dalton. He came to New York from Missouri to change his name from J. Frank Dalton back to "my christened name" of Jesse Woodson James, the celebrated outlaw.

He said he is 102 years old, that the alleged shooting of Jesse James by Bob Ford in St. Joseph in 1882 was a great hoax to permit his escape from the law, and that it actually was Charlie Bigelow who got a bullet "in the back of the head" from Ford's gun.

HE brought along six "corroborating witnesses" who believe fervently that he is the real Jesse; there's no doubt that he knows Jesse's operating terrain thoroughly—and the history of the "operations."

"There never was a James gang," the old man said as he lay in bed in his hotel room. "Ain't a farmer in the country—in those days—that wouldn't try to make a little more money if he got the chance. And that was the James gang.

"Let me tell you," he pointed his left index finger—a finger with the tip end shot off, "I'd usually maybe have two or three experienced men with me. But as the usual thing I'd go around to farmers before a robbery and I told 'em: 'If you want to go out and get a little piece of money—I don't know, say $50, $70, $100—you come with me and I'll take you and we'll get it. Didn't tell 'em what we were going to do. And we went.

THE latest Jesse lives at Meramec Caverns, Stanton, Mo., where Jessee James had a hideout during the Civil War. He suffered a hip fracture not long ago and is confined to bed. His right arm is paralyzed, from a stroke. He constantly fingers a bedside revolver with his left hand and says that as a boy he "used nearly a barrel of 'catridges' learning to shoot left-handed."

"I got $2,000,000 buried in the Wichita mountains near Fort Sill," the old man said. "There's been people lookin' for it, but never found it. If anybody gets it, let 'em get it the way I did."

DeWitt Travis, 61, an oil man, of Longview, Texas, who is helping "Jesse's friends" pay for bringing him and the witnesses to New York and for the petition in Union, Mo., circuit court to change Dalton's name, back to James, said he was "positive" this was the real Jesse. He said he sat on Jesse's knee as a young boy when the hiding Jesse stayed at the Travis home and has been associated with him for 30 years.

TRAVIS said the James boys kept his mother from starvation during the Civil War and that "Dalton" was always accepted in their home as Jesse James. Travis indicated he believed he could locate Jesse's hidden cache and said the $2,000,000 "will probably be handed back to the government when Jesse dies."

The latest Jesse James said he never wore a mask at robberies, but that he did wear false whiskers as a disguise. He told of taking a diamond ring from Jay Gould (his sworn enemy) in a train robbery, and Travis, who has the ring, said Gould's daughter, Helen, had identified it years later.

Dalton said he attributed his long life to "living in the open." He said if he had it all to do over again, he'd do the same thing. He said he'd have to because the government wanted Jesse for "treason" after the Civil War for belonging to Quantrell's guerrillas "and for treason you hang."

In St. Louis, Charles Van Ravenswaay, director of the Missouri historical society, said there had been about as many claimants to Jesse's name as there had to John Wilkes Booth's. He was inclined to doubt that anybody but Jesse was murdered by Ford in 1882 but said, after all, he couldn't be certain.

May 17, 1973

Dear Roy,

Glad to hear from you. There is an awful lot to be done. I doubt that we can do it in our lifetime.

Del Schrader says you know how to run or operate a magnetometer, which is a mighty good thing in my opinion.

Helping me around and over many states were, Roscoe James, Shortly James, Cowboy James, Russell James, Smith James and several dozen more.

Grandpa Jesse W. James and ex-president Jefferson Davis were amongst the men who founded several banks, one of which was the First National Bank of Colorado Springs. Of course, J. W. J. had to use an alias. The money came from down below Pueblo about two-thirds the way to Walsenburg, Colorado where it had been buried near a stage coach relay Depot at or near what has become known as Crow, just below Rye, Colorado.

Lots of gold was buried here in the way of secret rooms and tunnels under old Colorado City. I got one small treasure out at an old Chinese boardinghouse, later at a bottle works at 28th Street and at the creek where bottles were blown to help supply an old brewery on the creek.

Bob Ford was Jesse James chief bookkeeper when the old Standard Gold Mill and others were busy. Bob Ford's wife died there and his buried under the name, Florence Ford. J.W.J. had Bob Ford commute back-and-forth from Colorado City to Central City, Leadville to Butte, Montana, Salt Lake to Brigham Canyon, Utah. Bob also commuted back and forth from Colorado City at his main office near Rogans Saloon was located to Trinidad, Rotan Pass, Walsenburg, and Pueblo overseeing mine and smelter payrolls, taxes, management, etc.

These Ex-Confederate leaders founded banks, general stores, railroads, stage lines, flour mills, distilleries, cattle ranches, gold and silver mines, and other commercial enterprises. About one half of the overall profits they buried in gold and silver deposits to finance (on a cash basis) a second civil war. They considered that the more gold they could hoard and keep out of circulation--the harder they were hitting their enemies. These men considered themselves as loyal Americans, dedicated, sworn, God fearing patriots who knew the truth.

A lot of J.W.J.'s men were stationed across the country, though many were still down around Denver, Colorado Springs, Leadville, Salt Lake City, Merced, and El Monte, California. Only a few are now live who can help us. I was with J.W.J. for many years mostly in and around Texas and Oklahoma oil fields in the wild and woolly days. Give me a call so we can make some plans.

Kind Regards,   Jessie L. James "The Hawk"

A letter from Jesse James III

Dean's 'Buried Gold' Story Isn't New

JUL 1 1973

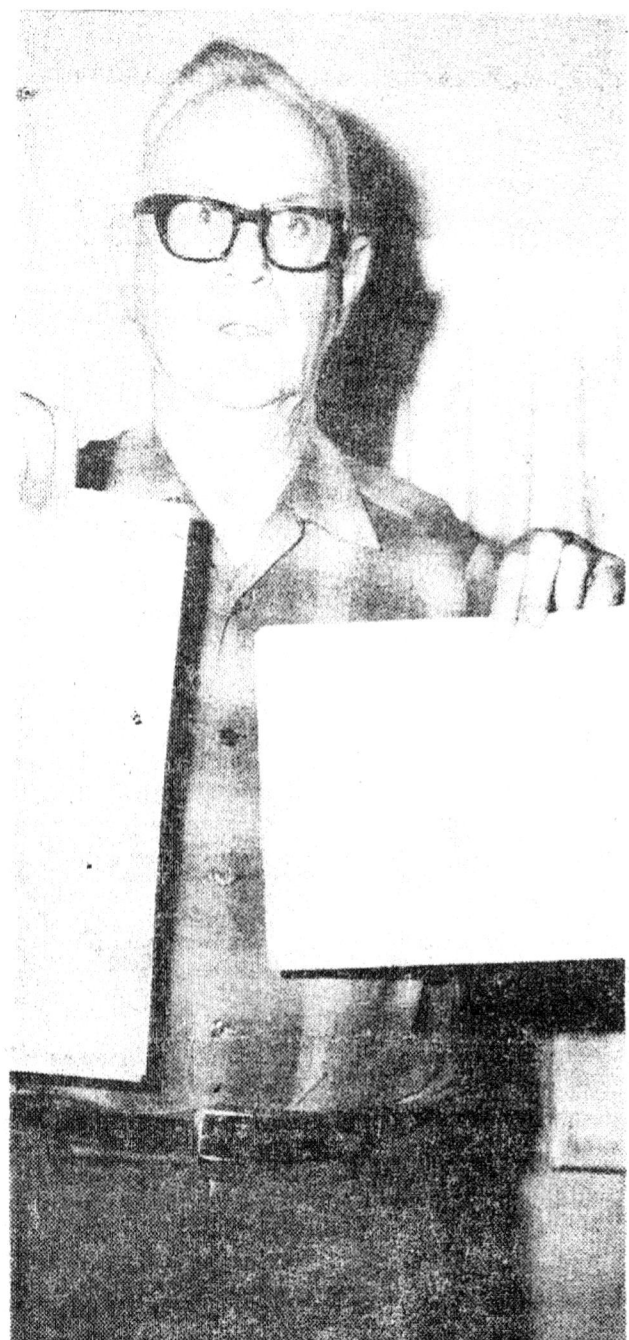

Herald-Examiner photo — Jesse James III, grandson of America's best known outlaw, holds up map and directions to buried Confederate gold in the Alamogordo area of New Mexico. James refuses to make any connection between his maps and the supposed buried gold referred to by John Dean in Senate testimony.

By DEL SCHRADER
Herald-Examiner Staff Writer

"Everything seems to be turning up these days in the Watergate hearings so I wasn't surprised this week when President Nixon's fired counsel, John W. Dean III, brought up the matter of buried treasure," Jesse James III of Banning said yesterday.

Dean testified that former Atty. Gen. John Mitchell told H.R. Haldeman, former White House chief of staff, at a luncheon Dean says he attended, "Criminal lawyer F. Lee Bailey has a client who has an enormous amount of gold in his possession and would like to make arrangements with the government whereby the gold could be turned over to the government without the client being prosecuted for holding the gold." Dean termed Haldeman "non-responsive."

According to Dean, Bailey's client or clients proposed to deliver 292 bars of gold, each weighing 80 pounds to the Treasury Department. The treasure allegedly was part of "an old Aztec cache" hidden on the White Sands, N.M., rocket range. Federal law prohibits U.S. private citizens from possessing pure gold, but placer gold is exempted

"In the first place," James told The Herald-Examiner, "it's not pure gold because the bars probably contain about 20 per cent zinc, copper and other minerals, but the treasure could be worth about $25 million at $42 an ounce. And it's not 'Aztec gold' — the old Confederates called it their Alamogordo Cache. It's just part of more than $500 million in Confederate gold buried in the state of New Mexico."

In a letter to the Treasury Department early in June, Bailey said his clients were "unsophisticated in dealing with government officials, and were suspicious of some future attempt to prosecute them if they tried to move the gold without government permission."

In a reply to Bailey, the Treasury Department reportedly said it "must be informed of the location of the gold and the circumstances of its discovery before it can pursue the case."

"This is a typical bureaucratic reaction," James snorted. "With our former European allies kicking around the value of the U.S. dollar, you'd think Washington would wake up. God alone knows how much gold may have been recovered from small Confederate caches and found its way to European and Oriental markets where it commands a much higher price."

James and other descendants of the Knights of the Golden Circle members last April disclosed the top Confederate spy organization from the end of the Civil War until 1916 amassed approximately $100 billion in treasure, burying it in depositories and caches in nearly every state in the Union. It was hoarded for a second Civil War, which never came.

Jesse III has definite ideas on what he refers to as "the gold mess." He said, "I believe the U.S. should compete in the International gold market by making use of the old Confederate treasures—letting the price seek its own level. When President Roosevelt made it illegal for U.S. private citizens to possess gold in 1934 it may have been unconstitutional, but he got away with it.

"Now gold, like Prohibition, has become a racket. If we outlaw handguns, a flourishing black market will spring up. Why sell gold to the U.S. government, however, for only $42 a troy fine ounce, when it has gone as high as $128.50 on the European market? Within a year, I predict gold will top $200 an ounce overseas."

The grandson of one of America's most notorious outlaws, Jesse III can sympathize with attorney Bailey and his clients. "I think they were trying to do the right thing and I think Haldeman was wrong in giving them short shrift. It set a dangerous precedent—now anybody who finds gold bars will do their best to smuggle them out of the U.S. because they know their government is hard-nosed and intractable. It will become a Boston Tea Party in reverse."

Using a map, Jessie III in 1961 located $704,000 in gold bars buried by his grandfather under a ledge on the Santa Clara Indian Reservation in New Mexico, but an Indian guide made off with the trove during the winter. A Federal Judge ruled the treasure belonged to James, but the moved gold bars were never found and four Indians were allegedly killed over the incident.

Following the much publicized court case, James recalls, "Several men who identified themselves as 'government officials' insisted I turn over all my secret maps of Confederate caches to them. At first I thought they were joking, but when they got nasty and serious, I told them which cliff they could jump off of.

"I may be wrong—and I hope I am—but Mr. Bailey and his clients may find their $25 million treasure isn't worth a plugged nickle. Greedy bureaucrats can always find a way to confiscate the trove."

"In essence, the Treasury Department is saying, 'Take us by the hand and show us where the money is and maybe, yes, maybe, we'll let you keep a farthing or two if you're good boys.' It's incredible how unrealistic and stupid our bureaucrats in Washington can be without half trying. They've lost touch with reality."

These are some comments by Jesse James III regarding the news story at the time when attorney, F. Lee Bailey was trying to get the US Government to purchase a huge amount of gold bars--treasure that was originally found in a hollow mountain (Victoria Peak) at the White Sands Missile Range in 1936 by Doc Noss. Noss succeeded in removing some of the bars, but was then murdered by his partner over it. After the military took possession of the area during World War II, the rest of the treasure was removed by parties unknown and mysteriously disappeared.

THE DENVER POST. OCTOBER 12, 1962

Badman's Kin Wins Right to Gold Cache

A Colorado man who claims he's a grandson of Jesse James has won a legal victory in his years-long fight to recover $600,000 in gold bullion supposedly buried by the famed outlaw.

U.S. District Court in Albuquerque this week ordered a Santa Clara Indian to deliver the bullion to the attorney for Jesse Lee James III.

James, who lives in Manitou Springs, insists that his badman-grandpa really wasn't gunned down by Bob Ford back in 1882, but instead lived to a ripe old 107. Badman Jesse died in Hood County Tex., on Aug. 15, 1951, the Colorado man says.

Jesse III has searched for years for 14½ gold bars supposedly buried by his grandfather in northern New Mexico. The bullion reportedly was gathered to finance a second Civil War to be waged by Southerners.

Jesse III claimed in his federal court suit that he learned where the bullion was buried, and that he had directed an Indian, Joe Suazo, to dig it up.

According to the suit, Suazo found the bullion—but promptly reburied it because "the spirits told me to do so." The suit charged that Suazo refused to divulge the new hiding place.

U.S. District Court ordered Suazo to turn over the gold to James' attorney.

Benard A. McCauley, who operates a Denver polygraph (lie detector) testing agency, said he examined the grandson last fall. Results of the polygraph tests indicated he was telling the truth, McCauley said.

This story seems to confirm that Jesse James III did actually know where some of the KGC treasure was buried. In this case, he says that it was buried by his grandfather, Jesse James, when he was a member of the KGC.

Los Angeles Herald-Examiner, Sunday, Apr. 22, 1973 A-3

$100 Billion in Treasure—
The Search for Rebel Gold

By DEL SCHRADER
Herald-Examiner Staff Writer

An incredible story of buried Confederate Underground treasure throughout North America with a dollar value of $36 billion at $35 an ounce or $100 billion on the Paris gold market was revealed this week in a small Riverside County town.

After the Senate recently voted 68-23 to permit Americans to buy, sell or own gold for the first time since 1934, I was invited to attend a "confabulation" of old "Confederates"—sons, grandsons or great-grandsons of the elite Knights of the Golden Circle, top Southern spy organization which closed its books in 1916 after more than a half century of existence.

The claimed $36 billion figure is impressive considering foremost geologists estimate the world's known yet recoverable gold reserve at 1 billion ounces. No estimates are available on Russia. U.S. gold production has been averaging about 1.5 million ounces per year during the last decade.

The Confederate Underground infiltrated gold mines around the world, causing false production figures. For half a century much gold was smuggled into the U.S., including $32 million from Afrikaners during the Boer War. Underground agents encouraged miners and stamping mill employes to steal and served as "fences," the oldtimers revealed.

A decade ago a national magazine writer charged that at least $50 billion in U.S. gold had "disappeared" since colonial days. At one time the U.S. Treasury listed $22 billion in gold reserves, but the vaults at Fort Knox, Ky., are bare by comparison today.

The oldtimers, who aren't "rednecks," racists or slavers, laid down certain conditions for my attendance. There would be no cameras or tape recorders allowed and no names, only initials must be used and all "off-the-record" statements must be honored.

I was given some of the depository maps, which I was allowed to make Xerox copies of. R.R.L. explained, "They won't do anybody much good. The maps are accurate as far as they go, but you'd need the two or three transparent overlays, which each fit into a landmark, for the specifics. In most cases, a vital point of reference is carved on a nearby rock."

Despite its famous Gold Rush, California ranks well down the line in hidden gold. Montana-Idaho reportedly contains $4 billion, Texas $2.5 billion; New York $1 billion and California has $500 million.

J.L.J. explains, "The amount varies from $41 million in Sacramento to $1.6 million in San Gabriel Canyon which is buried under a 90-foot-deep landslide and $250,000 in El Monte, which was a Golden Circle headquarters prior to the Civil War. Nevada City, Grass Valley and Placerville each have about $16 million and Porterville, $3.3 million. There are lesser amounts in Fort Tejon, San Diego, San Pedro, San Jose, San Francisco and Paso Robles."

Why the secrecy on the part of the oldtimers? They explain it by saying they vary from 67 to 91 years of age and have no desire for notoriety or even publicity. They all are either sons or grandsons of men who ranked high in the Knights of the Golden Circle hierarchy. They all grew up under the Golden Circle secret code which called on the nearest member to "kill without compunction or hesitancy" any other member who "betrayed the cause."

J.L.J., whose grandfather headed the Knights of the Golden Circle when it decided there wasn't going to be a second Civil War and shut down, said, "We are dying out fast and our story should be told, but all of us have been either shamed or disappointed by reporters in the past. They either broke confidences or failed to understand the story and ignored the salient parts. Or worse yet, they got it all botched up."

J.L.J. explained, "When General Lee surrendered to General Grant in 1865, the Yankee blockade had choked us off. The South was starving — but it still had at least $7 billion in well-hidden gold reserves."

"The Golden Circle, led by Gen. William C. Quantrill (really Elbert DeWitt Travis, brother of William Barrett Travis, who commanded the Alamo when it fell), and Col. Jesse James (outlawed by President Lincoln in 1863) almost immediately after Appomatox established a Confederate Underground capital in Nashville, Tenn., which flourished for 19 years.

> "Quantrill and James, along with 10 other members of the Inner Sanctum, vowed they'd beg, borrow and steal gold so that Civil War II, if it ever came, could be fought on a cash and carry basis ... many former Confederate officers profited and tithed up to 50 per cent of their annual incomes ..."

"Quantrill and James, along with 10 other members of the Inner Sanctum, vowed they'd beg, borrow and steal gold so that Civil War II, if it ever came, could be fought on a cash-and-carry basis and that international war lords and bankers would not realize usurous profits from blood lost on the battlefield. Many former Confederate officers headed West, profited and tithed up to 50 per cent of their annual incomes. Yet all hidden gold was offered — like the $33 million stolen from tycoon Jay Gould over a period of years.

"Now keep your pencil ready. For the first time a newsman is going to have the complete list of 12 that ran the Golden Circle. In addition to General Quantrill, who didn't die in a Union Army hospital in Kentucky in 1865, and Colonel James, the Inner Sanctum included Gen. Nathan B. Forrest, John Patterson (Jefferson Davis' alias), Gen. Bud Dalton, George Payne, Prof. B.E. Bedecsek, Lewis Dalton, George Baxter, Coleman Younger, Gen. J.O. Shelby and Jack (Brac) Miller. As members of the Inner Sanctum died, they were replaced up to 1916."

This writer was presented with a dozen snapshots of strange carvings on Western rocks. J.C.J. said:

"There are many outdoorsmen who believe all rock carvings were put there by the Indians. Well, let them think that because a serpent's head, bird or arrow might be pointing to a $14 million buried treasure. In the course of almost a century there have been floods, earthquakes and highways and cities have been built right over the caches. So the landscapes have changed."

J.L.L. volunteered: "My father told me the depositories or caches were located in the following areas: near state or territorial capitals, near railroad rights-of-way, along principal rivers, beside stage or wagon roads, around Confederate-owned livery stables, near old forts, near Catholic missions or cathedrals, near Indian agency headquarters, near bridge or ferry crossings, near smelters or mills and along natural landmarks like the Continental Divide."

"The Golden Circle spared no expense in burying its stolen or accumulated gold. It employed the best engineers and the most modern equipment. My Daddy said a white laborer was seldom employed in building a depository. Indians or Negroes were preferred because they could keep their mouths shut."

"Some of the caches might be safely opened by weekend treasure hunters, but don't trifle with the big depositories. They're all boobytrapped from all directions and more than one snooper has been blown into a million pieces."

Why hasn't the $36 billion (or $100 billion if sold in Paris) in treasure been removed before?

J.C.J. answered: "First, it couldn't have been touched until the last Confederate veteran died. That was in the Golden Circle Code. Second, only a handful of oldtimers have authentic maps of the depositories and in those that have been opened the gold has almost always been seized by the U.S. government as contraband. Third, the booby trap danger — the waterproofed explosives will still kill you! Last, but not least, President Roosevelt banned private possession of gold in 1934 when he raised the price from $20.67 an ounce to $35."

Will the Confederate oldtimers immediately move to open the depositories if the House follows the Senate action and President Nixon signs the private ownership of gold bill into law?

J.L.J. replied: "We'll first try to cut a deal with the U.S. government. Say, it would give us 10 per cent tax free and safe from the do-gooder bureaucrats. We'd take our 10 per cent and establish scholarships for the much-maligned Indians and descendants of Negroes and Mexicans who worked on our ancestors' depositories. We'd preserve historical landmarks. And we'd financially aid non-Communist pacifist groups because the Knights of the Golden Circle which amassed this fortune believed only war lords and international bankers profit from war."

J.D.J. said, "We have all the aces, kings, queens and jacks. We know how to get at the treasure — Washington doesn't."

Reached in Washington, D.C., Rep. Charles E. Wiggins, R-El Monte, said, "If the oldtimers can show us even a deuce or a trey regarding the treasure troves, we'll have something to go on." Wiggins is on the House Judiciary Committee.

J.L.J. revealed there's $500 million in "The Dakotas," $610 million in New Mexico, $350,000 each in Nevada and Utah, $1/2 million in Arizona, $600 million in Colorado, $333,000 in Oregon and $175 million in Washington, Canada contains billion, Mexico $500 million, $333 million in the New England states and $63 million in the Canary Islands. There are lesser amounts in nearly every state in the Union."

Are the oldtime Confederates trying to "blackmail" the U.S. government into a deal?

J.L.J. smiled: "Not at all. The gold can just lie down there until doomsday, I guess. With our devalued dollar and poor balance of payments situation, Washington could use this long-forgotten gold. We'll give it to them — but we believe we deserve 10 per cent for a finder's fee if nothing else."

$60 MILLION HERE? Old rock symbol is said to point to cache near Four Corners in Utah.

$40 MILLION HERE? Master Compass treasure in New Mexico is reported near this guide rock.

$250,000 HERE? Bird atop figure's head points the way to New Mexico cache, oldtimers say.

$100,000 HERE? Missing right arm, raised left hand denote nearby horde in California desert.

What looks like ordinary Indian carving on this Utah rock and the other rocks above are actually directions in code denoting locations of caches and contents, according to a group of oldtimers whose grandfathers served in Confederate army.

This old sketch is among hundreds purportedly passed down to descendants of Confederate officers who claimed to have buried huge hordes of gold all over the country. Horizontal shaft was dug deep into the side of a hill near a river and gold cache planted. Oldtimers claim the cache is heavily boobytrapped by still potent explosives and that a series of transparent overlay maps is needed to get full details on the location, near Cat Den Butte in western Texas.

Dels story on the KGC. (See following four pages for blow-ups.)

By DEL SCHRADER
Herald-Examiner Staff Writer

An incredible story of buried Confederate Underground treasure throughout North America with a dollar value of $36 billion at $35 an ounce or $100 billion on the Paris gold market was revealed this week in a small Riverside County town.

After the Senate recently voted 68-23 to permit Americans to buy, sell or own gold for the first time since 1934, I was invited to attend a "confabulation" of old "Confederates" — sons, grandsons or great-grandsons of the elite Knights of the Golden Circle, top Southern spy organization which closed its books in 1916 after more than a half century of existence.

The claimed $36 billion figure is impressive considering foremost geologists estimate the world's known yet recoverable gold reserve at 1 billion ounces. No estimates are available on Russia. U.S. gold production has been averaging about 1.5 million ounces per year during the last decade.

The Confederate Underground infiltrated gold mines around the world, causing false production figures. For half a century much gold was smuggled into the U.S., including $32 million from Afrikaners during the Boer War. Underground agents encouraged miners and stamping mill employes to steal and served as "fences," the oldtimers revealed.

A decade ago a national magazine writer charged that at least $50 billion in U.S. gold had "disappeared" since colonial days. At one time the U.S. Treasury listed $22 billion in gold reserves, but the vaults at Fort Knox, Ky., are bare by comparison today.

The oldtimers, who aren't "rednecks," racists or slavers, laid down certain conditions for my attendance. There would be no cameras or tape recorders and no names, only initials must be used and all "off-the-record" statements must be honored.

I was given some of the depository maps, which I was allowed to make Xerox copies of. R.R.L. explained, "They won't do anybody much good. The maps are accurate as far as they go, but you'd need the two or three transparent overlays, which each fill in a landmark, for the specifics. In most cases, a vital point of reference is carved on a nearby rock."

Despite its famous Gold Rush, California ranks well down the line in hidden gold. Montana-Idaho reportedly contains $4 billion, Texas $2.5 billion; New York $1 billion and California has $500 million.

J.L.J. explains, "The amount varies from $41 million in Sacramento to $1.6 million in San Gabriel Canyon which is buried under a 90-foot-deep landslide and $250,000 in El Monte, which was a Golden Circle headquarters prior to the Civil War. Nevada City, Grass Valley and Placerville each have about $16 million and Porterville, $3.3 million. There are lesser amounts in Fort Tejon, San Diego, San Pedro, San Jose, San Francisco and Paso Robles."

Why the secrecy on the part of the oldtimers? They explain it by saying they vary from 67 to 91 years of age and have no desire for notoriety or even publicity. They all are either sons or grandsons of men who ranked high in the Knights of the Golden Circle hierarchy. They all grew up under the Golden Circle secret code which called on the nearest member to "kill without compunction or hesitancy" any other member who "betrayed the cause."

J.L.J., whose grandfather headed the Knights of the Golden Circle when it decided there wasn't going to be a second Civil War and shut down, said, "We are dying out fast and our story should be told, but all of us have been either shamed or disappointed by reporters in the past. They either broke confidences or failed to understand the story and ignored the salient parts. Or worse yet, they got it all botched up."

J.L.J. explained, "When General Lee surrendered to General Grant in 1865, the Yankee blockade had choked us off. The South was starving — but it still had at least $7 billion in well-hidden gold reserves."

"The Golden Circle, led by Gen. William C. Quantrill (really Elbert DeWitt Travis, brother of William Barrett Travis, who commanded the Alamo when it fell), and Col. Jesse James (outlawed by President Lincoln in 1865) almost immediately after Appomatox established a Confederate Underground capital in Nashville, Tenn., which flourished for 19 years.

> "Quantrill and James, along with 10 other members of the Inner Sanctum, vowed they'd beg, borrow and steal gold so that Civil War II, if it ever came, could be fought on a cash and carry basis... many former Confederate officers headed West, profited and tithed up to 50 per cent of their annual incomes..."

"Quantrill and James, along with 10 other members of the Inner Sanctum, vowed they'd beg, borrow and steal gold so that Civil War II, if it ever came, could be fought on a cash-and-carry basis and that international war lords and bankers would not realize usurous profits from blood lost on the battlefield. Many former Confederate officers headed West, profited and tithed up to 50 per cent of their annual incomes. Not all hidden gold was pilfered — like the $32 million stolen from tycoon Jay Gould over a period of years.

"Now keep your pencil ready. For the first time a newsman is going to have the complete list of 12 that ran the Golden Circle. In addition to General Quantrill, who didn't die in a Union Army hospital in Kentucky in 1865, and Colonel James,

$100 Billion in Treasure— The Search for Rebel Gold

the Inner Sanctum included Gen. Nathan B. Forrest, John Patterson (Jefferson Davis' alias), Gen. Bud Dalton, George Payne, Prof. B.E. Bedeczek, Lewis Dalton, George Baxter, Coleman Younger, Gen. J.O. Shelby and Jack (Brac) Miller. As members of the Inner Sanctum died, they were replaced up to 1916."

This writer was presented with a dozen snapshots of strange carvings on Western rocks. J.C.J. said:

"There are many outdoorsmen who believe all rock carvings were put there by the Indians. Well, let them think that because a serpent's head, bird or arrow might be pointing to a $14 million buried treasure. In the course of almost a century there have been floods, earthquakes and highways and cities have been built right over the caches. So the landscapes have changed."

J.L.L. volunteered: "My father told me the depositories or caches were located in the following areas: near state or territorial capitals, near railroad rights-of-way, along principal rivers, beside stage or wagon roads, around Confederate-owned livery stables, near old forts, near Catholic missions or cathedrals, near Indian agency headquarters, near bridge or ferry crossings, near smelters or mills and along natural landmarks like the Continental Divide."

"The Golden Circle spared no expense in burying its stolen or accumulated gold. It employed the best engineers and the most modern equipment. My Daddy said a white laborer was seldom employed in building a depository. Indians or Negroes were preferred because they could keep their mouths shut."

"Some of the caches might be safely opened by weekend treasure hunters, but don't trifle with the big depositories. They're all boobytrapped from all directions and more than one snooper has been blown into a million pieces."

Why hasn't the $36 billion (or $100 billion if sold in Paris) in treasure been removed before?

J.C.J. answered: "First, it couldn't have been touched until the last Confederate veteran was dead. That was in the Golden Circle Code. Second, only a handful of oldtimers have authentic maps of the depositories and in those that have been opened the gold has almost always been seized by the U.S. government as contraband. Third, the bobby trap danger — the waterproofed explosives will still kill you! Last, but not least, President Roosevelt banned private possession of gold in 1934 when he raised the price from $20.67 an ounce to $35."

Will the Confederate oldtimers immediately move to open the depositories if the House follows the Senate action and President Nixon signs the private ownership of gold bill into law?

J.L.J. replied: "We'll first try to cut a deal with the U.S. government. Say, it would give us 10 per cent tax free and safe from the do-gooder bureaucrats. We'd take our 10 per cent and establish scholarships for the much-maligned Indians and descendants of Negroes and Mexicans who worked on our ancestors' depositories. We'd preserve historical landmarks. And we'd financially aid non-Communist pacifist groups because the Knights of the Golden Circle which amassed this fortune believed only war lords and international bankers profit from war."

J.D.J. said, "We have all the aces, kings, queens and jacks. We know how to get at the treasure — Washington doesn't."

Reached in Washington, D.C., Rep. Charles E. Wiggins, R-El Monte, said, "If the oldtimers can show us even a deuce or a trey regarding the treasure troves, we'll have something to go on." Wiggins is on the House Judiciary Committee.

J.L.J. revealed there's $500 million in "The Dakotas," $630 million in New Mexico, $330,000 each in Nevada and Utah, $175 million in Arizona; $500 million in Colorado, $333,000 in Oregon and $175 million in Washington, Canada contains billion, Mexico $500 million, $333 million in the New England states and $63 million in the Canary Islands. There are lesser amounts in nearly every state in the Union."

Are the oldtime Confederates trying to "blackmail" the U.S. government into a deal?

J.L.J. smiled: "Not at all. The gold can just lie down there until doomsday, I guess. With our devalued dollar and poor balance of payments situation, Washington could use this long-forgotten gold. We'll give it to them — but we believe we deserve 10 per cent for a finder's fee if nothing else."

$60 MILLION HERE? Old rock symbol is said to point to cache near Four Corners in Utah.

$40 MILLION HERE? Master Compass treasure in New Mexico is reported near this guide rock.

$100,000 HERE? Missing right arm, raised left hand denote nearby horde in California desert.

$250,000 HERE? Bird atop figure's head points the way to New Mexico cache, oldtimers say.

What looks like ordinary Indian carving on this Utah rock and the other rocks above are actually directions in code denoting locations of caches and contents, according to a group of oldtimers whose grandfathers served in Confederate army.

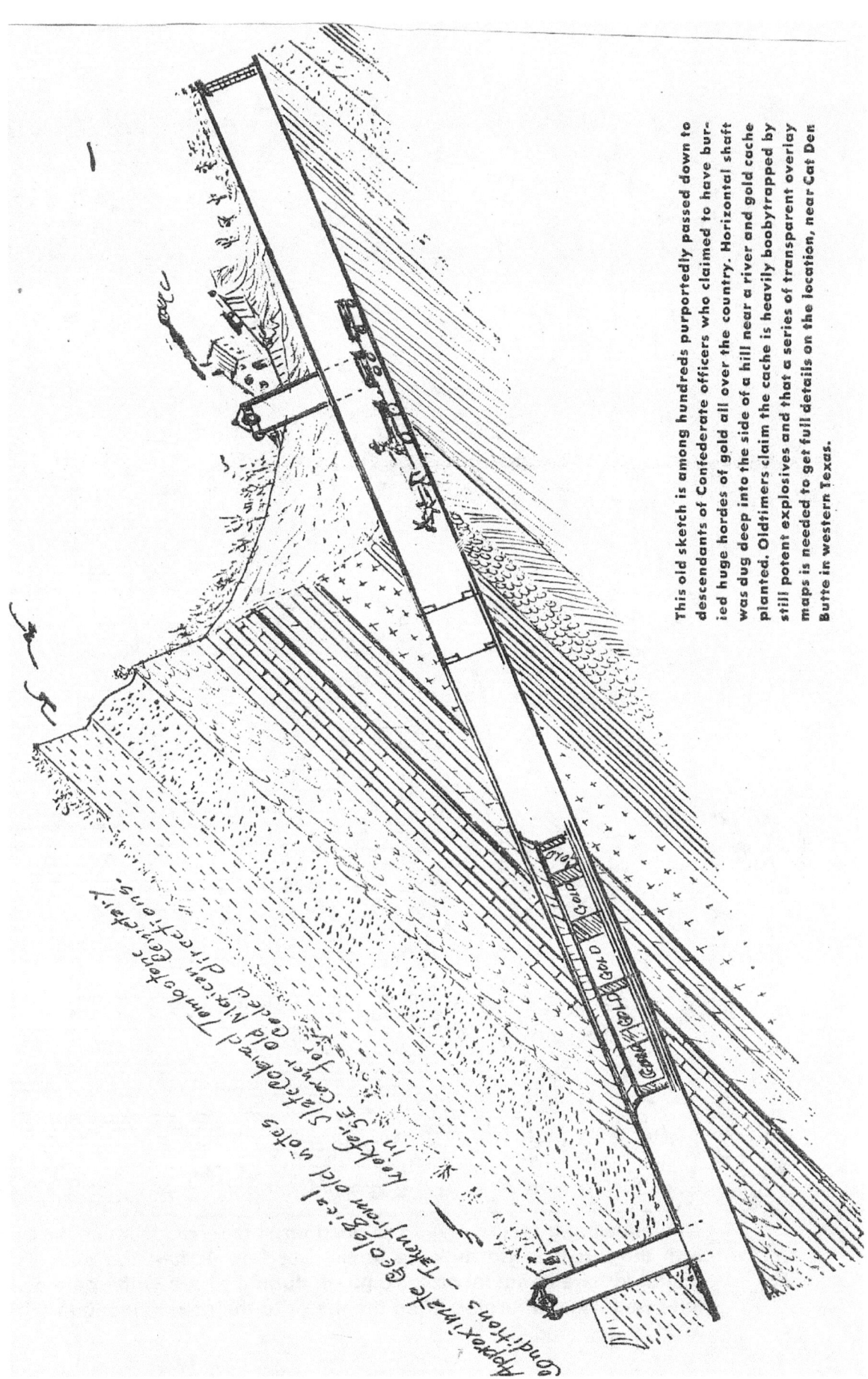

This old sketch is among hundreds purportedly passed down to descendants of Confederate officers who claimed to have buried huge hordes of gold all over the country. Horizontal shaft was dug deep into the side of a hill near a river and gold cache planted. Oldtimers claim the cache is heavily boobytrapped by still potent explosives and that a series of transparent overlay maps is needed to get full details on the location, near Cat Den Butte in western Texas.

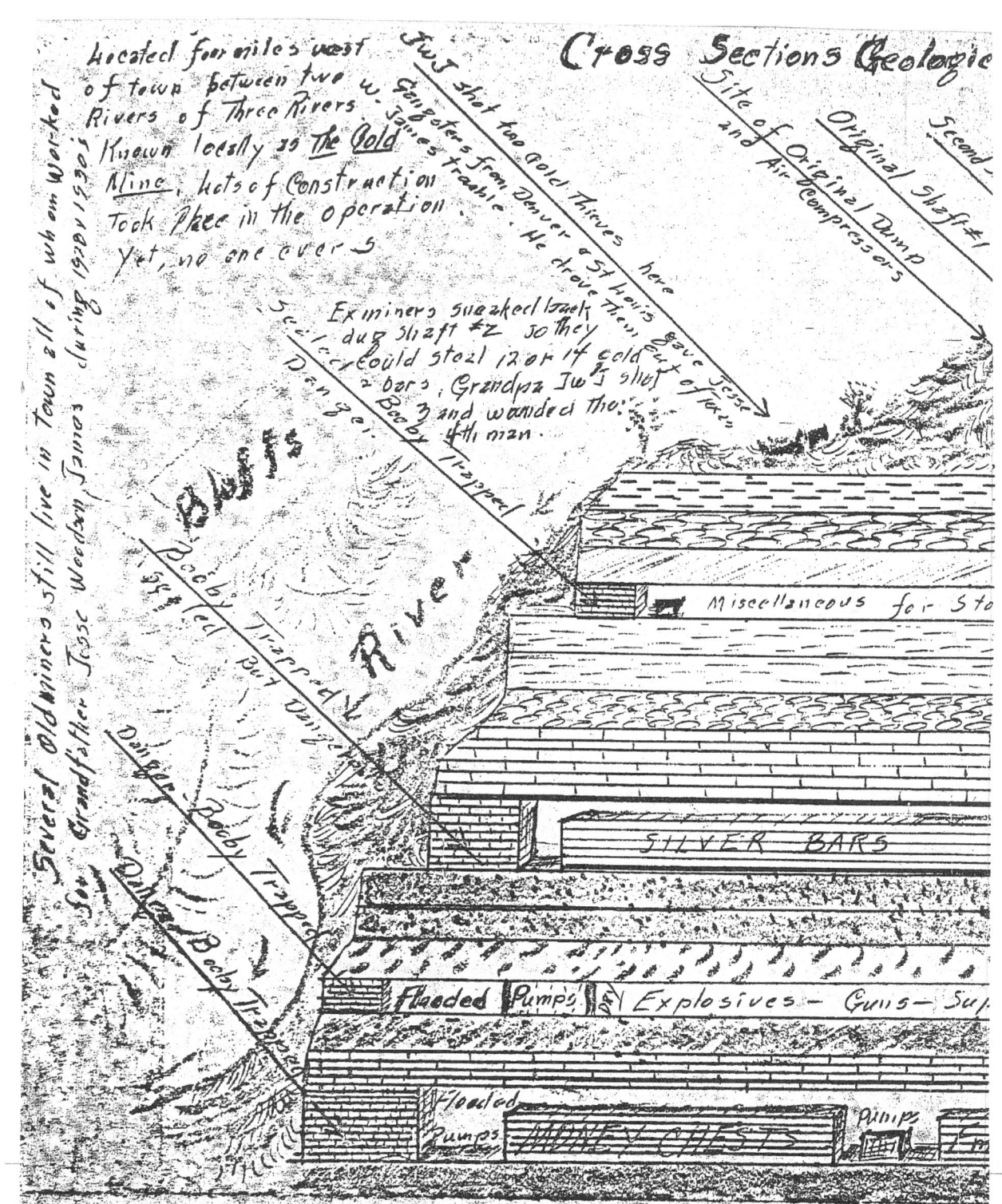

The following treasure maps are ones that I received from Jesse James III with the intent to go look for some, but I never had the time. They are reprinted here in actual size, some on double pages with some over-lap. I have no further information on them, nor to their exact location other than what is indicated.

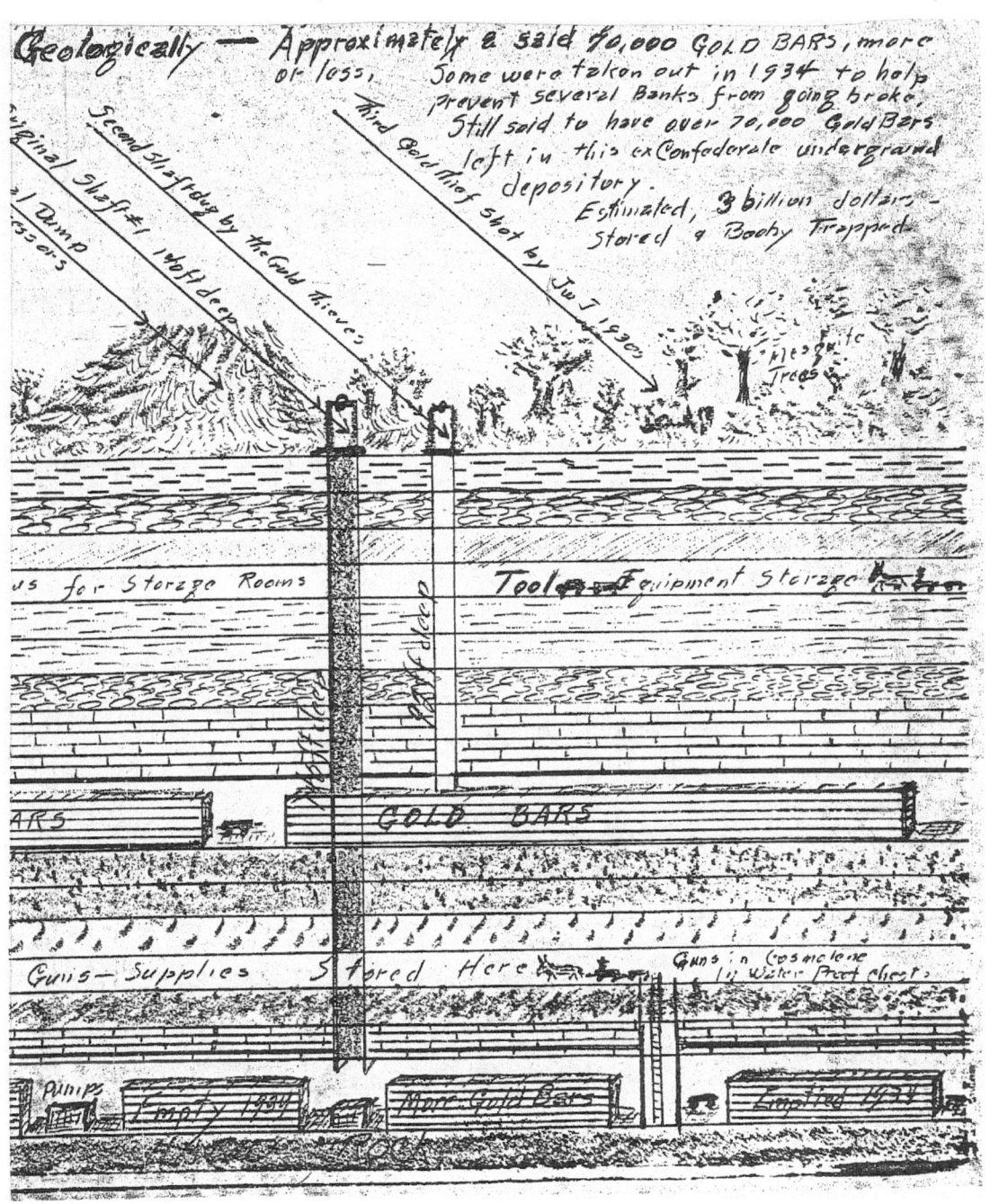

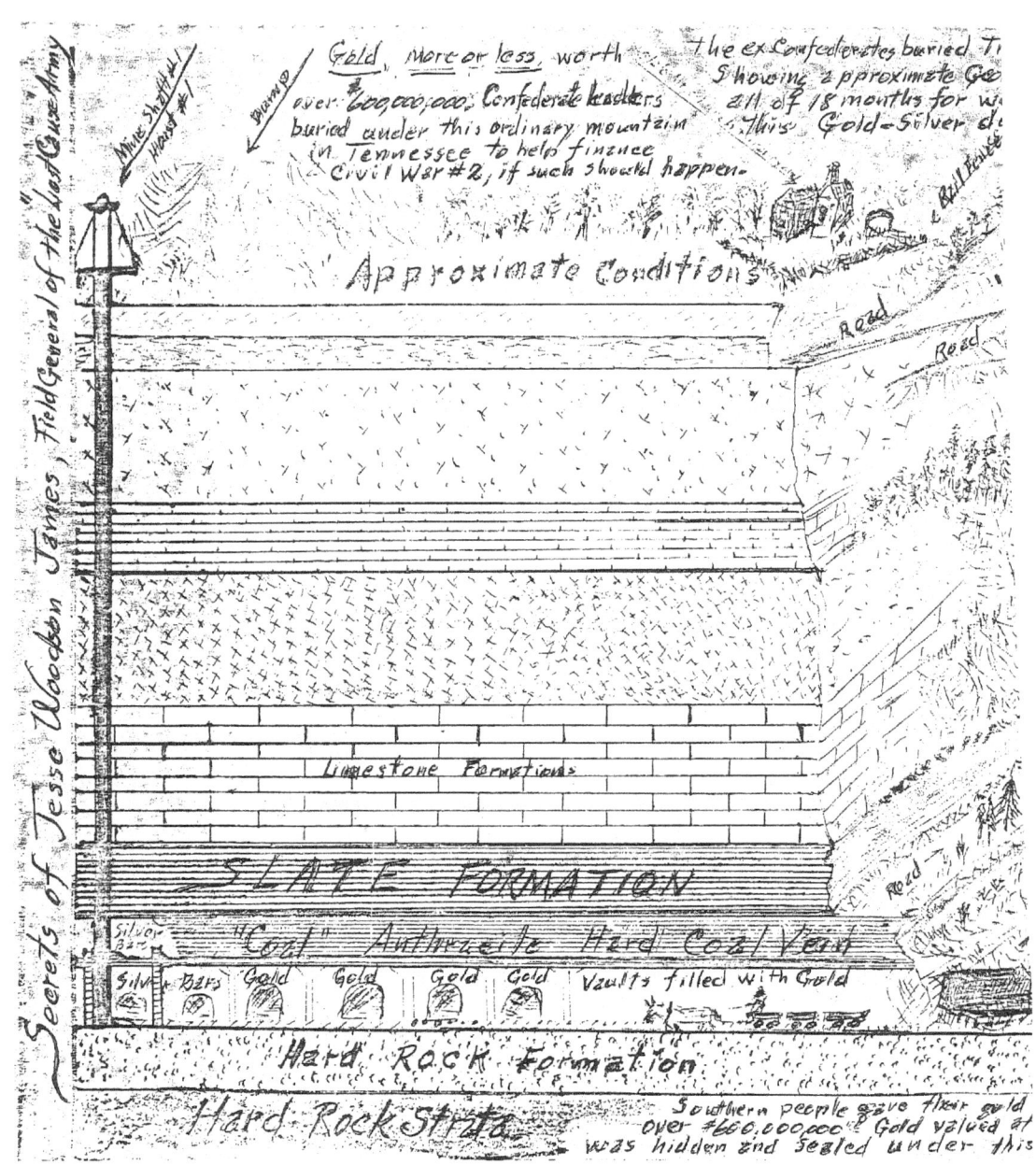

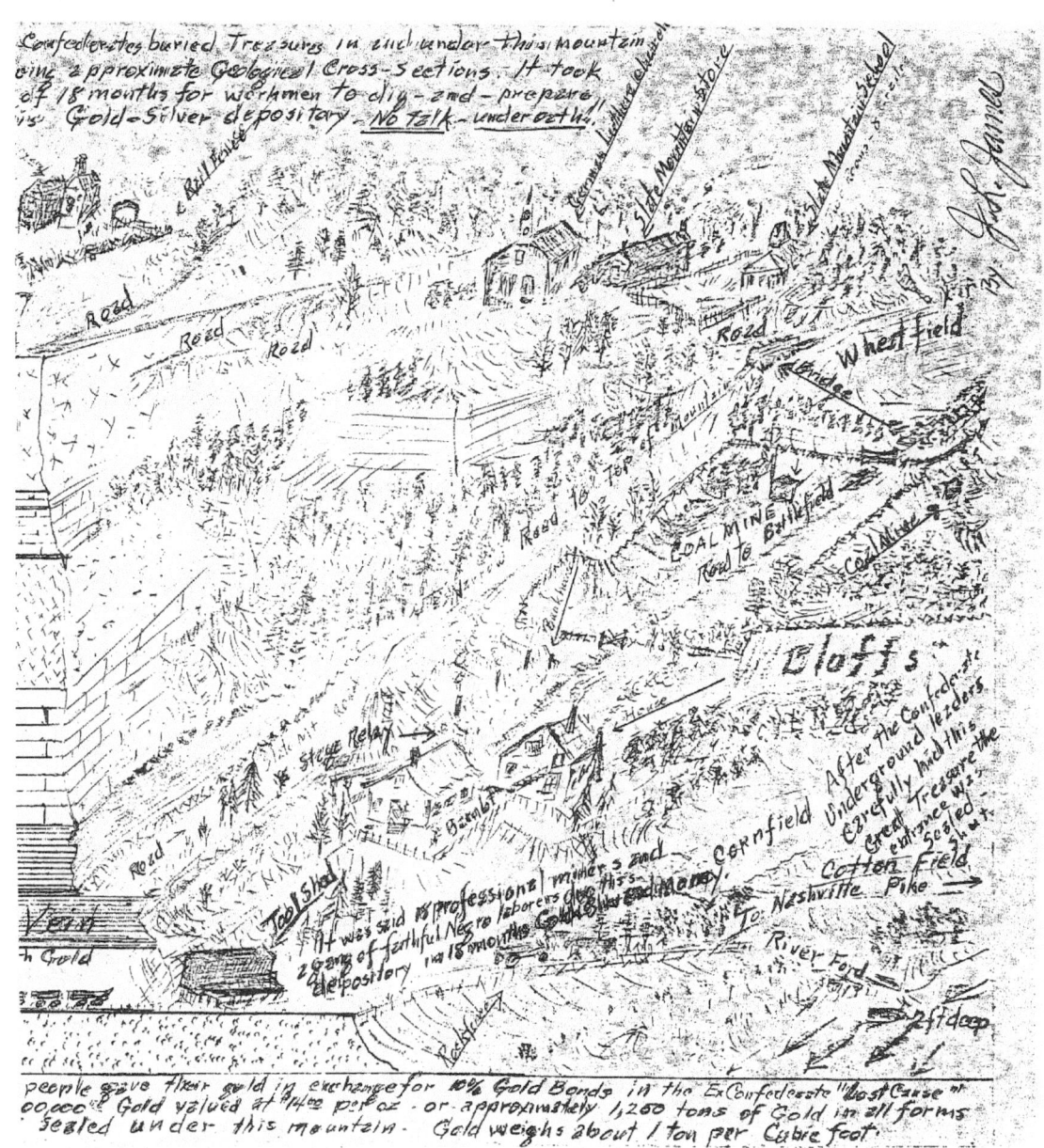

In 1869 Jesse W. James rode all the way from Malad City, Idaho, to lead the ex-Confederate raiders in the capture of a said 66 tons of Gold dust and nuggets, known as placer Gold. The Markers are similar as herein Shown -

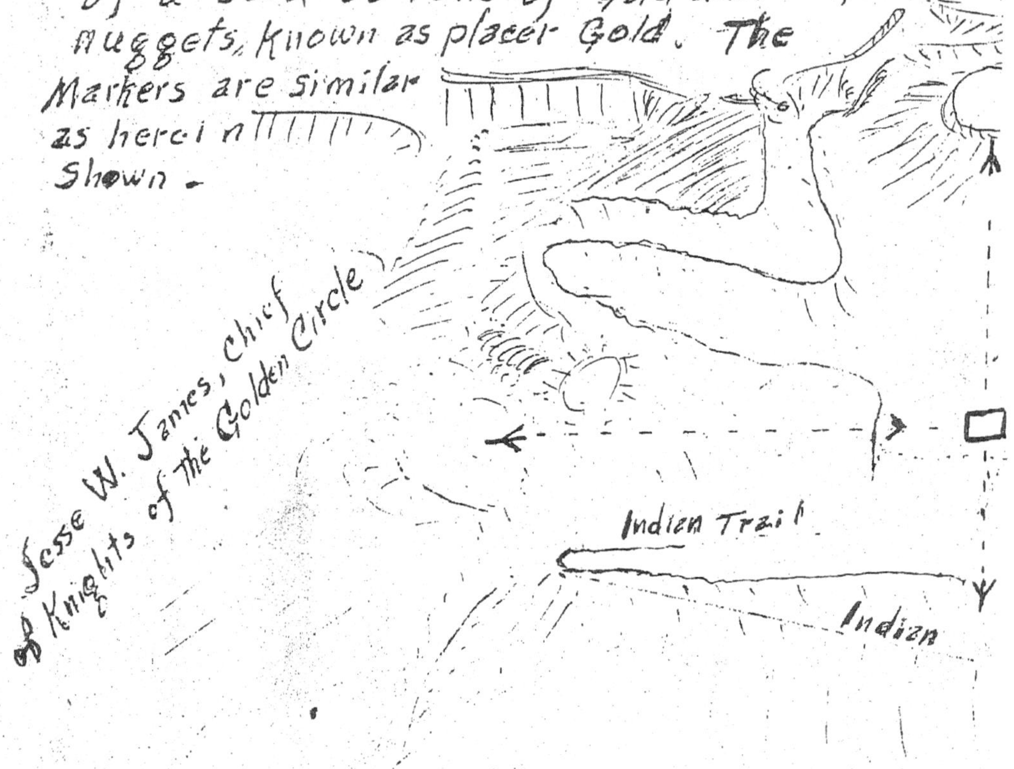

Jesse W. James, chief of The Knights of the Golden Circle

Indian Trail

Indian

This gold was said to be an accumulation of gold in

Information from Ex-Confederate Army Officers were involved in the capture and Robbery from Granite, to Denver, Colo., in 1869. and Silver Money was hoisted up an old

A Tombstone at S.E. Corner of Fairplay Colorado.

'll The
ead the
ture
nd

The Legend was current and known as "The Vanishing Wagon Train." It complety vanished into Apparent Mystery. Not a Trace was ever found. Not even a Mule or Horse nor Oxen was ever found.

Treasure 22ft deep Hid'd under big Slabs of rock

Elevation: 13,000 ft. Above Sealevel

Indian Trail

This Chart is Almost Exact. Only a few points to be added - as Complete

N↑ E→ W←

gold in over ten years — To be shipped To Europe.

Officers and surviving Laborers & Gunmen who Robbery of a whole Wagon & cart train bound 1869. A said 66 tons & some good deal of Gold an old Indian Trail. buried 22 ft deep.

The Treasure of the Curious Mule in the Rocky Mountain remote County of about 1885-86 Confederate buried Gold mines mostly placer Gold - several tons of Gold - Gold Bars etc.

After a few tons of placer Gold was hoisted into the cave just as the dam was about completed, more gold was floated to the cave and stored there in - while the water level was maintained at the level of the cave's floor. Once these men had stored the said gold safely they then backed about 20 more feet of water up and over the roof of this cave as you now see this chart. The symbol painted on the wall with pigment and Prussic Acid is a water-bug who's tail points at a downward slant to this cave - mostly placer Gold and some rough gold bars.

Figure of the Curious Mule

A simple symbol points to the cave plus the symbol of the Water Bug

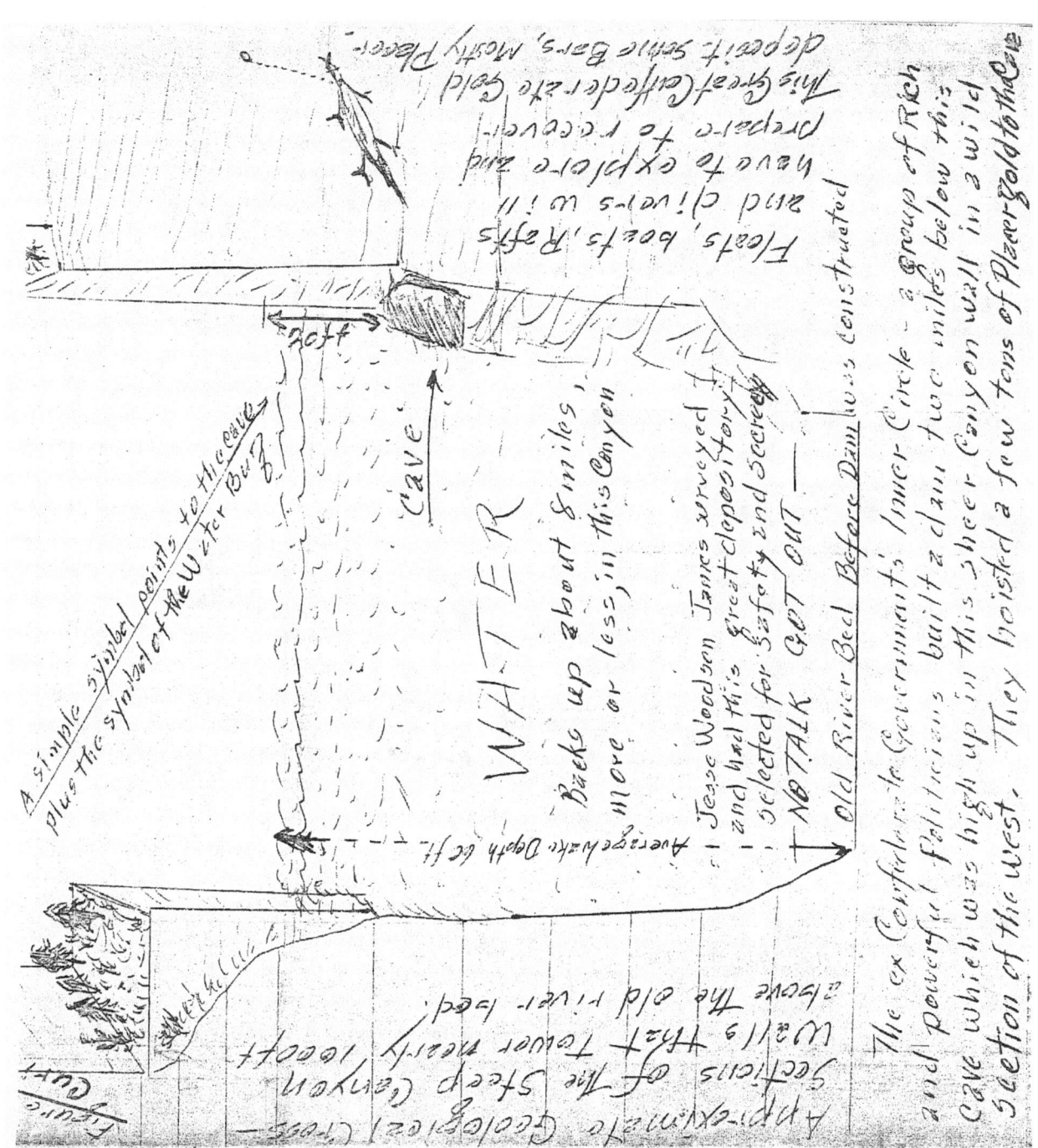

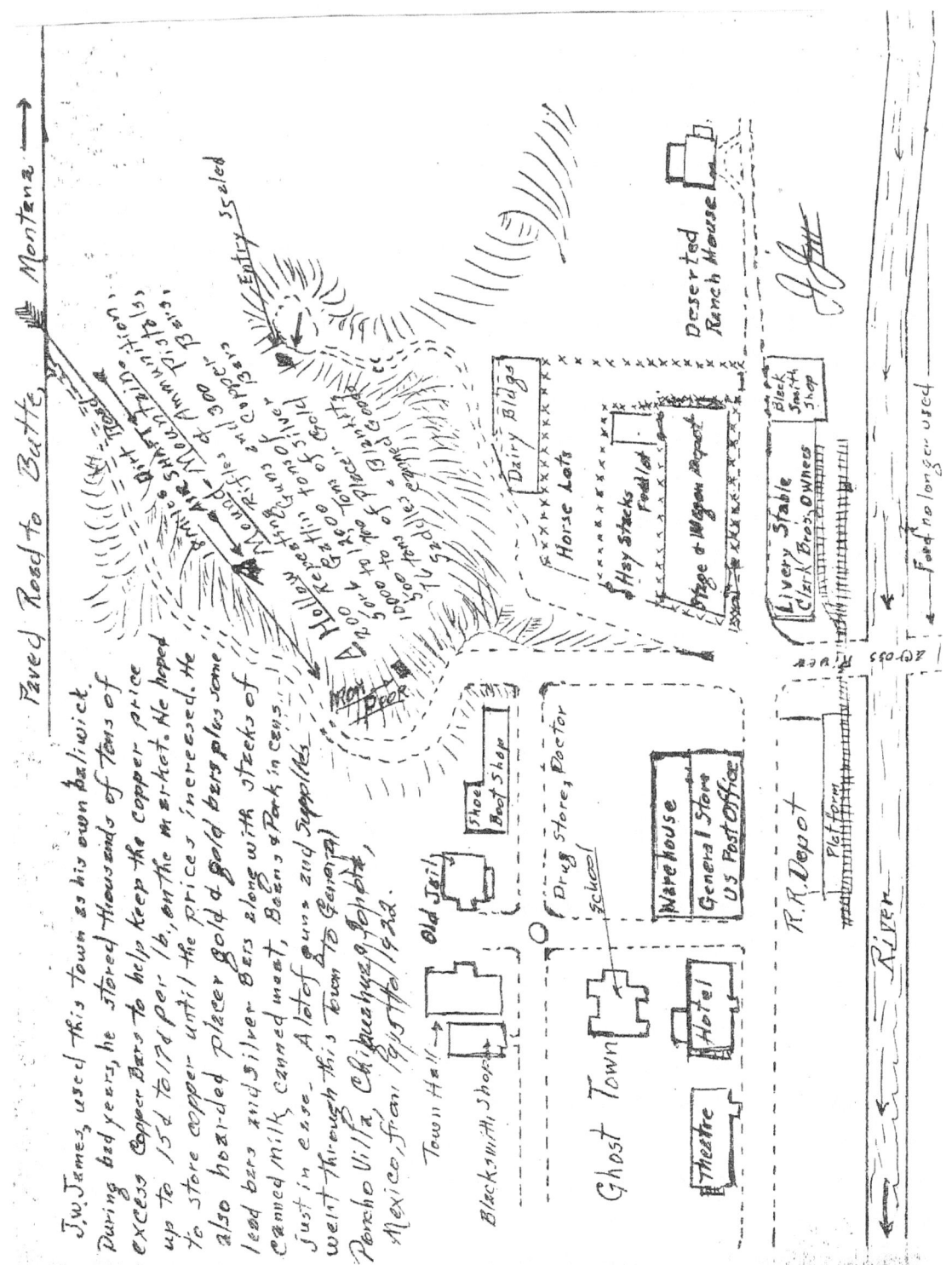

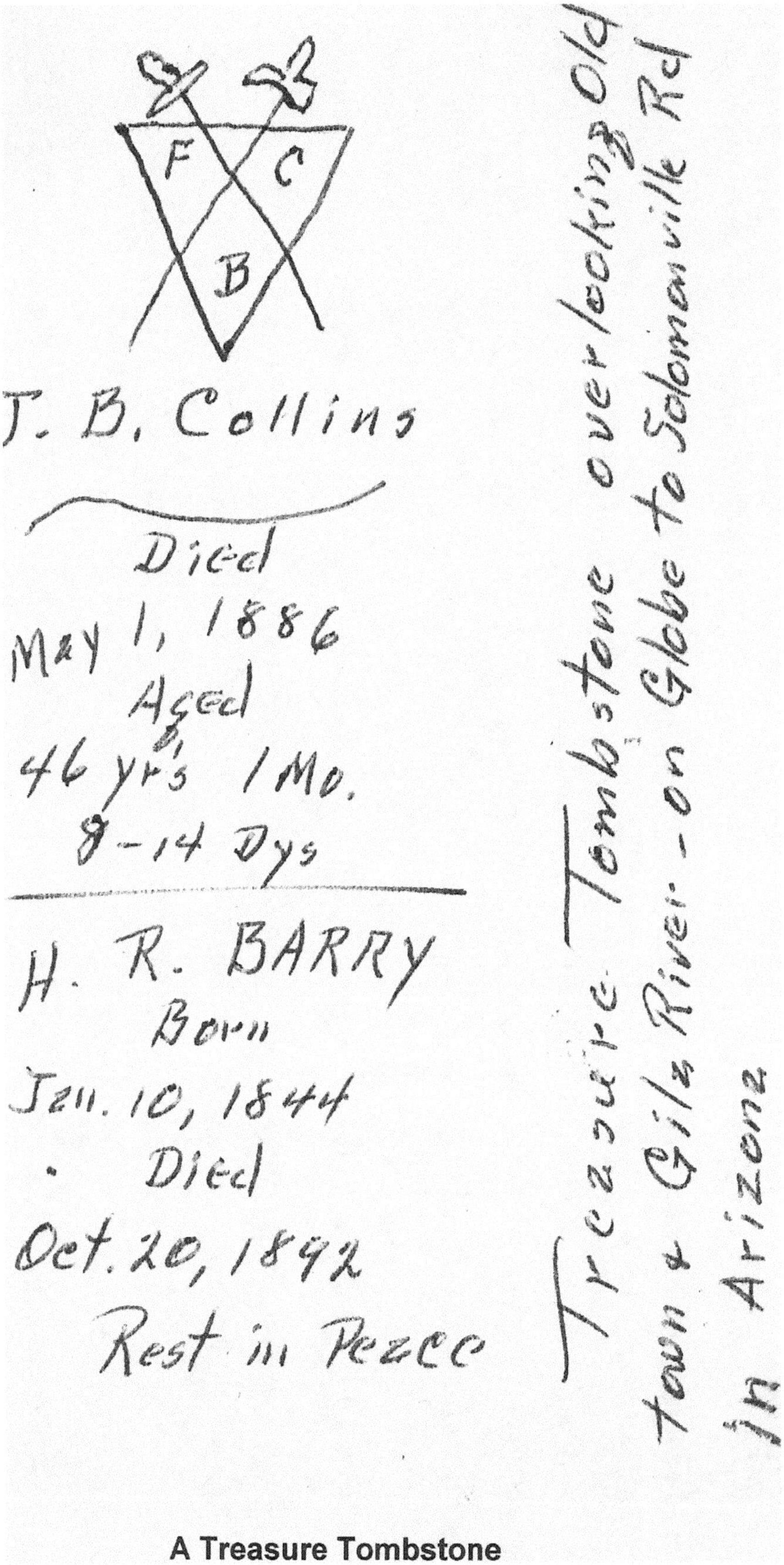

T. B. Collins
Died
May 1, 1886
Aged
46 yrs 1 Mo.
8-14 Dys

H. R. BARRY
Born
Jan. 10, 1844
Died
Oct. 20, 1892
Rest in Peace

Treasure Tombstone overlooking Old town & Gila River - on Globe to Solomonville Rd in Arizona

A Treasure Tombstone

Well, we were taught by ex-Confederate leaders that Jefferson Davis, his wife and daughter didn't go back to Mississippi - the story goes they left Virginia by boat, landed several places along the Atlantic Seaboard just long enough at each landing to unload cargo — passengers, mail, etc etc., and cargo taken aboard. What the general public didn't know was — many millions of dollars worth of CSA GOLD was placed in the hold of the sail ship. It took on some gold, we were told at Tampa, Mobile, then landed safely at New Orleans. At New Orleans a sternwheel riverboat was ready. So, the Gold was moved at night along with the Jeff Davis Family, servants and bodyguards — quietly sailed up Mississippi River, to land and unload at Jefferson, Texas. A huge pile of hollowed out cypress logs were already prepared. Since express wood was used to make the best rowboats & flatboats no nosey Carpetbaggers even remotely suspected what those hollowed out cypress logs actually contained nor that Jefferson Davis was any where else but in the State of Mississippi.

Once the laborers placed all the gold in hollow logs the next problem was roll them over a pile them onto three huge log wagons. One had ten yoke while the other two had 18 yoke of oxen pulling them — they were extremely heavy.

They left the Caddo Lake landing about 1 1/4 miles south of Jefferson, Texas, to Marshall, Texas, turning west. They were thoroughly checked at a carpetbagger checkpoint and toll gate as the three heavily loaded log wagons slowly rolled toward Longview. At long view they were again closely inspected by a Union Army Cavalry Patrol at the edge of town. It was explained that these 30 foot long cypress logs were to be used constructing a toll bridge farther west on Sabine River. This route went through St. Clair (Gladewater) Big Sandy, Mineola, Lynwood, Willspoint to Old Cyene, Texas, the logs for the most part, would be used for piling.

Little did the Yankee checkmen realize that one of the ox-team drivers was President Jefferson Davis, going by the alias of "John Patterson", baggy clothes, worn out boots, battered felt hat wielding a long whip with a pepper that sounded like pistol shots when he expertly cracked that long blacksnake whip. Nor did the Yankee Carpetbaggers and Cavalry Patrols even dream that on those three huge log wagons was hidden nearly 2 billion dollars in gold. Gold is very very heavy said to weigh almost 2000 lbs. per cubic foot. These logs plus the GOLD hidden-in-them made hauling them by oxen a stove-pipe cinch, they were not going more than 10 to 14 miles per day. Meantime from up north possibly Denison, Texas, three huge iron Safes hauled on three more wagons were to meet Jeff Davis log wagons at SALTMARSH.

Hidden from the road, in the woods the three safes were made ready and the cypress logs stacked at the edge of the salt marsh. That year one of those periodical droughts was in progress. So three holes were dug in this salt marsh, hollow logs opened and the gold was re-weighed, entered into a ledger, tabulated, valued, safes were sealed and by block-and-tackle were carefully lowered into the holes then covered-up — brush was piled on the filled-up holes and set afire. The logs were used, for the most part, to construct a toll bridge in the vicinity. In a few weeks rain came along in September, the salt marsh became it's usual shallow, boggy feeding place for wild ducks and geese. Many noted, famous men took refuge in what was known as "The Free State of Van Zandt" which surrounded such towns as Canton, Myrtle Springs, Grand Saline, etc., etc.

The Jefferson Davis' Confederate Treasure Depository, somewhere in East Texas' FREE STATE of VAN ZANDT.

Jeff Davis III — BOGGY — Marsh — Dangerous
Quick Sands
When full of water

|Fill|Fill|Fill|
|GOLD|GOLD|GOLD|

JEFF DAVIS

Three Huge Safes rest on bedrock in a Salt Marsh which hold the JEFF DAVIS GOLD DEPOSITORY, another Strategic Military location of the Confederate Underground Army

P.S.

I may notify you to fly down & assist us on the 3 huge safes in East Texas, #1 Jeff Davis safe, #2 Cole Younger safe, #3 Jesse W. James' safe all buried in a triangle just inside a swampy area & if dry days set-in we may tackle them late this summer. These were personal features of all three men.

Hit this current cache right on the nose but problems with sand, water & mud — we already took a lot of iron & steel out of the hole exactly as Prof., said.

JJ

This is a most interesting and rare old photograph of two rather famous old westerners given to me by Jesse James III. It is of Ora Goodnight (left), a nephew of Colonel Charles Goodnight, the Texas cattle baron; and Frank "Pistol Pete" Eaton who I often saw in Enid, Oklahoma during the late 1930's while I was in school there. He looked then exactly as he does here—long braded hair, Mustache, cowboy boots with spurs, scarf, cowboy hat, and a .45-Colt Revolver that he always wore, loaded—even in town. He never had a car, but would ride his horse into town and tie it up to a parking meter. He had a long reputation as a gun fighter and the police never bothered him. In fact, they treated him as a celebrity and often visited with him. He was quite an attraction and a noted trick-shot artist. He only had one eye, but every Cherokee Strip Celebration, he would put on a shooting exhibition in the public square to the amazement of everybody. As a young boy on a ranch, he had witnessed his parents and a sister being robbed and killed by a party of four or five men. He swore he would hunt them down some day and kill them all, which he did. But first, he had to take lessons from the gunfighters of the day, including those stationed at Fort Gibson east of Tulsa--the "Top Gun" school" at the time. Then he carried out his vow, getting wounded only once. Later, he worked for many years as a gun hand for the famed Cattlemen's Association to keep law and order in the West. He later wrote a book, entitled "Pistol Pete" that I still have a copy of. So, what Jesse James III had to say about him, I knew to be true.

The author's collection of Metal Detectors. Each one had different features.

The author's special team of treasure hunters in New Mexico searching for the famous "17 Tons of Gold" hidden there in 1931 by Mexican Nationals, hoping to sell it to the United States Mint, but failed to do so. The hunt was filmed by the Tokyo Broadcasting System.

Chapter Four

A Treasure Hunt To Glorieta Pass, New Mexico

It took a few months after meeting the man who said that he was Jesse James III, before we were ready to go look for the treasure at Glorieta Pass. But first, I had to check on who owned the land. It was then that I found out that my old friend and treasure hunter, Bill Mahan, had a treasure hunting lease on it. So, I contacted him at his factory in Garland, Texas where he was manufacturing the D-Tex Metal Detector. It was one of the very first on the market. He had also published one of the very first magazines on the subject of treasure hunting.

He gave me written permission to proceed and to keep anything that we found. Apparently, he had been there before, but he said he had not found any treasure. In a way, I thought it lent some credence to Jesse James III's story that it was indeed a treasure site. Bill was one of the first to tell me about the treasures of the Knights the Golden Circle back in about 1970; but of course, like others at the time, I thought that the existence of the group and their treasure was a rather far-fetched tale. But, I had learned to always keep an open mind.

We arrived at the location early one Sunday morning after spending the night in Santa Fe, New Mexico about 18 miles away to the northwest. We immediately broke out the metal detectors and set out searching. Jesse had not drawn a sketch for us. He only said to watch for "Turkey tracks."

I asked, "What are Turkey tracks?"

He replied, "Watch for things that are not supposed to be there, or things that are not natural."

It rather puzzled Del, but for me that was enough to go on--not only because of my experience in searching for treasure and their signs, but also I had spent half of my young life on a farm in Kansas, Oklahoma and Colorado, so I had a pretty good idea as to what was natural and what was not.

When we arrived, the first thing that caught my eye was a rather large, white, bull's-eye painted on the side of a very large rock on the east side of the road. Then, on the other side of the road, I noticed a rather large face that had been carved on a huge rock outcropping. It was about 20-inches in size and looked very much like the face of a jack-o-lantern. I noticed that the face was smiling which I took as a good sign. It also was looking towards the bull's-eye that was about 300 yards away on the other side of this small and shallow valley. Upon closer examination of the face, I could see that it was very old, perhaps 100 years, or more, and it had lichen growing on it. Since these two man-made objects were on opposite sides of the road and facing each other, that seemed to be telling me to start searching in the area between them.

I gave Del one of my extra metal detectors and showed him how to use it. Then I got out my favorite detector, a VP-200, which actually was a late model military mine detector like they were using in Vietnam. It was extremely powerful and had cost me a lot of money, about four times more than the most expensive detectors available on the commercial market. I soon began to pick up dozens of items from the Civil War battle that had been fought there in 1862 between a Union Regiment from Colorado and a Confederate Regiment from Texas. In fact, Santa Fe had been the Confederate Capitol of the West for about six months preceding the battle.

Among the items I found were a lot of .58-caliber mini-balls. These were the bullets used by both sides during the Civil War for their muzzle loading rifles. They were over one-half-inch in diameter and did a lot of damage when they hit. I also found a lot of casings from 4-inch cannon balls that had exploded. Many of them contained little lead pellets about the size of marbles that flew out in all directions with devastating results. I also found pieces from equipment, such as from wagons and harnesses.

SOME CLUES

As I was searching around the big rock outcropping where the stone face was, I noticed something unusual. Normally, I wouldn't have given it a second thought, except I suddenly remembered what Jesse James III had mentioned, which was to watch for something unusual and this was it. Here was an old tree about 100 years old, or more, about nine-inches thick that had two bends in it of about 90-degrees each. I could easily see that it had purposely been arranged like that when it was a young tree. Trees never grow that way on their own. I took a picture of it with John McFarland standing beside it. Now, I was beginning to get excited. It was placed just south of the huge rock that had the stone face on it. The tree must be part of the treasure signs I was to look for.

Excitedly, I began searching all around the area and also along the base of the huge rock. As I did, I discovered a small opening at the base at ground level by my feet. But since it was too small (about six-inches in diameter) it was too small to use my V-200 metal detector. So I switched to another detector I had with a four-inch loop. It fit well and I pressed it into the hole. It went back about a foot, then went on even further back another two feet.

"Wow!" I thought, "Could this be the hiding place?"

However, to my disappointment, there was no signal from the detector which indicated that nothing metallic was in the hole. Now, I got more curious. I pulled the metal detector out, took my flashlight, got down on my stomach and looked in. It was empty! However, I could see that it was not a natural hole. It was man-made, obviously by a drill of some kind since the sides were nice and smooth.

But since it was empty, I wondered if the treasure had already been recovered there. However, it really seemed a bit too small to have contained much treasure anyway. But who put it there at that location, and why?

As I stood there scratching my head and looking down at my metal detector that I had inserted into the hole again, I noticed that it had been made at a 45-degree angle. I thought that was strange. Why drill a hole at 45-degrees when a 90-degree hole would be easier to make?

"Hum," I thought. "Could this be telling me something?"

I took another look. Then it occurred to me that maybe it was pointing at something. I turned and looked in the direction where it seemed to be pointing out over the small valley below. When I did, my heart almost stopped!

There it was in plain sight…three very old and large pine trees, all the same height standing straight up (not bent) and in perfect alignment with each other and also in line with where the metal detector handle was pointing. Had a rifle been fired from the hole, it would have passed directly over the center of all three trees. Also, I noticed that there were no other trees of their size in the whole area--nothing but small scrubs and bushes. This could not have been a coincidence. There was meaning to this, especially when I noticed that the distance between the first and second tree was exactly twice the distance between the second and third tree. So, one tree was missing to make them all equal distance apart.

Eureka! The treasure must be where the missing tree would have been. Yes, that had to be it. It seemed perfectly obvious now. All these man-made signs now made sense. Excitedly, I rushed down towards the trees. I first searched around the base of the first tree which produced nothing. So, I headed for where the missing tree would have been. However, I had to detour a ways to my right to go around a rather deep dry wash with steep sides that blocked my path. I went to the last tree and paced off the distance back to the second tree. This gave me the distance I would have to walk towards where the missing tree would have been. It led me in a straight line (back towards the first tree) to a location about three feet from the edge of the deep dry wash that I had just detoured around. A tree at that spot would have made the distance equal between all four trees.

THE DISCOVERY

Where the missing tree would have been, I immediately started getting a strong signal with my VP-200 from something made of metal about two or three below. I started digging, then I could see that a large hole had been dug here once before and the dirt had been filled back in. About two feet below the surface, my shovel started scraping on the top of a large, rusting, but still intact, metal can. In the meantime, I had called out to my friends that I had found it and they were on their way.

It turned out to be large black-powder can. I recognized it as the kind that had contained black powder once used for muskets, cannons, and for blasting during mining operations during the last century. It was about 12-inches across and approximate 10-inches deep. I had seen many of them before lying around some of the old mines that I had explored. I hesitated. Now, I had to be careful. This could possibly be a booby-trap that I had been warned about. Nevertheless, I very carefully pried off the lid to look inside.

When I did, I discovered it was completely empty. Nothing! Why? Why? That just didn't make any sense. Why would someone go to the trouble of burying it there if it was empty and if it wasn't a booby-trap either? It was then that I realized that it was just a decoy to discourage any treasure hunter from digging any further. Of course, the people who put it there were crafty enough to have figured that out. So, the real treasure must be buried somewhere below. I hurriedly removed the can and started to dig further on down. Again, I could see that the dirt was a bit softer and a hole had been filled in here many years before. My heart was really pounding this time because I knew I was digging down to treasure!

About that time, John McFarland approached my location from the far side of the wash. He stopped when he got to the edge of it opposite from me.

Then he called out, "Roy, better not dig there anymore!"

"Why?" I shouted back. "Is there a booby-trap down there?"

He only repeated emphatically what he had said before, then added, "Better come over here and take a look at what is underneath you."

That gave me a bit of concern. Perhaps I was about to dig into a real booby-trap. I stopped digging immediately and walked around to where he was standing. Now, I could see why he said to stop digging. What we saw was where a recent flood had undercut the area directly below the powder can, and about three or four feet below the can was the distinct impression where a small chest or box had been. It had been approximately 18-by-20 inches in size...even a few small pieces of rotting wood was left. It could have actually been a military pay chest exactly like Jesse James III had claimed it would be.

The treasure was gone! It had been washed away in a very recent flood. Greatly disappointed, we just stood there and stared at the site for a while. Then, Del showed up and looked. All three of us could see what had happened.

Then to my surprise, both Del and John started getting paranoid and rather panicky to quickly get out of there. It scared them when they realized that this was indeed an actual treasure site which apparently had belonged to the Knights of the Golden Circle and that armed sentinels may still be watching it.

They both arranged their snub-nosed .38-revolvers to a position for a quick draw and hurriedly started for the car about a quarter-mile-away-- yelling something like, "Let's get out of here, now! Someone probably has a gun on us."

"OK. Now really, guys. Calm down." I said.

But they didn't seem to listen. They only hurried for the car and started loading up the trunk. I hardly had time to catch up with them. I also wanted to go back to photograph the location. But they said they didn't have time for that, and if I wanted to go along, get ready to leave...right then. I regret to this day that I didn't get a photograph of the location.

As we were loading up, a highway patrol car pulled up behind us. He was ignoring us--just doing some paperwork. But I did have time to go over to ask him a question. (I guess Del and John were feeling a little better with an armed officer on the scene.) I had noticed that someone had been living in the old Pigeon Ranch building directly across the road from us for some time and apparently had been giving personal tours of the battlefield. I had noticed some crude, hand-made signs posted around the area giving some details of the battle that had taken place at each of these locations. The signs were still there, but nobody was living there anymore. That had aroused my curiosity. The officer was very courteous and answered my question.

THE MAN WHO HAD FOUND THE TREASURE

"Oh, yes. You mean the old guy that used to live here? (He did mention the name, but I do not recall what it was.) Well, this summer we had a very heavy rainstorm here that lasted for days--one of the heaviest that we've had for years. When it was over, we got concerned about him and came to see how he was, but he was gone. When he didn't show up later, we put out an APB (all points bulletin) on him. Finally though, we did locate him. He was living in Albuquerque, and strangely enough, he seemed to be living high on the hog!"

So ended my first experience with searching for that treasure of the Knights of the Golden Circle. I could have told the officer why the man had been living high on the hog, but I didn't have time. They were honking the car horn for me to come immediately, and the car belonged to them, not me. On the way home, I remember thinking about the note that I had received from Bill Mahan giving me permission to search on the property and to keep anything that we found. In retrospect, I believe that he had already discovered that the treasure was no longer there.

Could there have ever been a treasure map for this location? No, I don't think so. There's always a problem with a treasure map, which is that it could be stolen or fall into the wrong hands. All that was necessary here, as it is probably true with many other sites, was to go to the location, look for treasure signs just like I did, and eventually be led to where the treasure was. Anyone looking here didn't need to believe that there were hidden meanings to the symbols since I don't think there were any here that were universally used, except for the bent tree. You just needed to use your head and see what each sign was trying to tell you. For example, the drilled hole in the rock that pointed to the three trees where the treasure was. Later, I recalled that the bent tree also pointed directly to where the treasure had been, as well as the smiling stone face. It all added up correctly.

So, this time I didn't find treasure, but at least I had the satisfaction of knowing that I had the skill and patience to find the treasure signs, decipher their meanings and to find the location where the concealed treasure had been. What a different story it would have been if I had learned of the treasure a few months earlier. It would have been ours and I could have retired from aerospace. This experience obviously lent credence to the KGC treasure stories that Jesse James III had been talking about.

Twice before, I had found where treasure had been, but I had arrived too late. A few years earlier, I had found where treasure had been in the front yard of a house north of Tulsa, Oklahoma where the mother of the famous outlaws, the Younger brothers, had lived until she died. She was a sister to the mother of Frank and Jesse James; so the Younger brothers were first cousins to Frank and Jesse James, and they had often worked together on some of their big robberies.

Working on a tip and with permission of the owner, I started searching with my VP-200 metal detector. Realizing that if someone buries a treasure near their house, they would always put it in a location where it can easily be watched from a window of a room that is occupied most of the time. I spotted the perfect place in the side yard where two huge boulders were that had a space of about three feet between them. From a window in the front room and also one from the kitchen, you could see all the space between them, like it was a little pathway.

I had no sooner started searching when I picked up a strong signal right in the middle of the pathway. Sure enough, just as I had suspected, this would have been the logical place. I put the detector down and started digging. About eight-inches down, I started uncovering the top to a rather small trunk with a rounded lid. It was obviously a very old trunk and it had been there for many years. My heart started pounding. I was getting close to a heart attack from the excitement! Then, the lid collapsed as I tried to open it. It was then that I could see that whatever was inside, had long ago been removed. Apparently, this had served as sort of a bank. It had been buried just deep enough for the lid to be covered so that one could quickly dig down to it to open the lid and place items in or take them out quickly, then cover it up again. How convenient it had been…but I was many years to late.

A few years before that, in the old ghost town of Searchlight, Nevada, located about 60 miles south of Las Vegas, in the center of the floor of a big house on the hill overlooking the town, I discovered a trapdoor that opened up to a large hole underneath where a small safe had once been. This had been the living quarters of the mining superintendent and it was here that he had kept the payroll for the minors. Again, I was years too late.

Then, there was a time when I was hired by two ladies to search for a treasure in the Elysian Park area of Los Angeles--a treasure that their father had searched for many years before. They led me to a certain hidden ravine where I soon discovered some carvings in some rocks and one rock that was shaped like a small tombstone. This led me to a place nearby where I discovered where an old tunnel had been dug, then filled in many years before. The treasure was supposed to be old Spanish or maybe pirate treasure, but it could have been from the Knights of the Golden Circle. I got a team together and we dug quietly for many nights, then concealed the area when we left. We did not want visitors. After digging 18 feet, we discovered where something very large and heavy had been removed many years before. We only found the remains of a very large and old rotting rope that had broken from the weight of removing the treasure. The story was shown for many years on the television program "Unsolved Mysteries."

But good treasure hunters are not discouraged by near misses.

Page 1   JOINT-VENTURE AGREEMENT

The undersigned parties, Jesse Lee James, 1011 E. 9th St., Beaumont, Calif.; Roy W. Roush, 425 N. Sycamore Ave., Los Angeles, Calif.; John R. McFarland, 11305 Hallwood Drive, El Monte, Calif.; and Del Schrader, 1613 Sixth Ave., Arcadia, Calif., hereby mutually agree to engage in and carry on, as joint venturers, for profit the herein below described enterprise, to be known as The Glorieta Cache, all pursuant to the terms and conditions hereof:

1. <u>The Enterprise</u>: The specific enterprise is the location, salvage and recovery of a cache of coins which had a value of $165,000 when buried in Glorieta, N.M., following the Civil War by John James, one of Jesse Woodson James' 19 brothers and sisters. By rule of thumb, Jesse Lee James estimates current market value to be about $1,650,000.

2. <u>Contributions</u>: It is Jesse Lee James' wish that the undersigned venturers share-and-share-alike in the profits of The Glorieta Cache. It is James' belief that a grubstake of about $15,000 must be raised. The rule of thumb for pay back on grubstaking is five-to-one, but any of the undersigned venturers are authorized to negotiate a pay back of $100,000 for an investment of $15,000. Communications on grubstaking must be maintained with the other venturers. Any unused monies from the grubstake will be returned to the grubstaker. Negotiations at the site will be handled by Mr. James, who believes from $5,000 to $10,000 will be needed to satisfy the owner of the property. The plan would be to fly to Albuquerque, rent a car with N.M. plates and proceed to the site, thus attracting less attention from the curious.

3. <u>Title to Property</u>: The parties' interests in the property recovered and produced as the result of this enterprise shall be as follows:

Jesse Lee James--	25 per cent;
John R. McFarland--	25 per cent;
Roy W. Roush--	25 per cent;
Del Schrader--	25 per cent.

4. <u>Division of Profits and Losses</u>: Any and all profits of the parties shall be divided under terms of Paragraph 3, but after an agreed-upon equal division, the majority of the monies shall be placed in a sinking or trust fund for future ventures in the joint names of the parties in this agreement. Moreover, any profits sustained from this venture shall be net after any and all possible State and/or Federal treasure trove laws are satisfied and/or legal fees or other expenses pertinent to retrieving The Glorieta Cache. Losses and/or expenses shall be sustained from grubstake monies.

See page 2.

This was our "Joint-Venture Agreement" that the four of us signed before we went to look for the Knights of the Golden Circle treasure at Glorieta Pass, New Mexico. We were not able to raise the "$15,000 grub stake" so we went without it and shared the expenses ourselves.

JOINT-VENTURE AGREEMENT

5. **Storage and Valuation of Recovered Items:** All items shall be prudently appraised and then disposed of by a most prudent but not necessarily hasty plan mutually agreeable to the venturers.

6. **No Assignment Without Consent:** No transfer or assignment of a party's interest in this joint venture or profits thereof shall be effective except with the express written permission of the other venturers.

7. **Necessity for Goodwill and Secrecy:** The parties to this Joint Venture Agreement stipulate that secrecy is mandatory for the execution of a successful enterprise and that as few people as possible be brought into the enterprise or discussion thereof. The undersigned agree to abide by the admonition: "Keep the lip buttoned."

8. **Effective Date and Term:** Effective date of this agreement shall be today, July 24, 1973, and this agreement shall continue in force until its terms are fully carried out or until determination by the venturers that The Glorieta Cache is unretrievable.

Executed at El Monte, California, July 24, 1973:

Jesse Lee James
Jesse Lee James

Roy W. Roush
Roy W. Roush

John R. McFarland
John R. McFarland

Del Schrader
Del Schrader

Treasure Talk with Bill Mahan

TO WHOM IT MAY CONCERN:

THIS NOTE ENTITLES THE BEARER, ROY ROUSH, AND PARTY
TO SEARCH ANYWHERE ON THE PIDGEON RANCH AND TO
KEEP ANYTHING HE MAY FIND.

WILLIAM A. MAHAN

Before we went on the trip, I researched to find out who I needed to get permission from. It turned out to be my old friend and fellow treasure hunter, Bill Mahan in Texas, who had a treasure hunting lease on the property. Bill had been a successful treasure hunter most of his life and was the manufacturer of D-Tex Metal Detectors, one of the first ones on the market. He also published a very fine and popular treasure magazine.

ARCADIA, CALIF. 91006

July 29, 1973

Dear Roy:

A somewhat incredible day at Beaumont. As we drove up, a car was just leaving Jesse's. Sarah Snow had just been visiting Jesse III. Who is Sarah Snow? Why, she's the daughter of Missouri Frank James! At about 91, she is dying of terminal cancer. Three months to live. I've read her book and letters, but how I would have liked a photo of Sarah and Jesse III.

You should have heard Jesse and John McFarland piecing together events of 50 years ago! I believe Jesse III knows more about John's father's ranch in Nebraska than John does. (I'm kidding--but Jesse has one of the best minds I've ever arm-wrestled).

I've told John he must work hard to come up with the $15,000--but I'm thinking we might end up financing the thing ourselves, Roy, and negotiating a split with the ranch owner. I know Jess doesn't want this approach, but we may be forced to it.

Today, Jesse said, "If we hit a dry hole at Glorieta, not far from there Grandpa buried $500,000 not far from the Santa Fe tracks. I can't put my foot on it like at Glorieta, but I know the area where it is located and I think between me reading the signs and Roy's gear we can find it."

Oh, Eddy Atkins is supposed to be at Jesse's next Sunday. I feel Jesse wants us there for moral support. At this meeting, Jesse is supposed to sign the papers for the Curious Mule and give him an exact map. Previously, Jess said, "I'd like to have Roy go up and ride herd on my interest." My feeling is that I'll believe Atkins is coming when I see him in person.

I don't think small, Roy, but I think the Glorieta Cache would put us in business. If we can work with John and Jesse, I think we could knock off quite a string of caches and might some day feel up to tackling a boobytrapped depository.

Will let you know soonest on grubstaking endeavors. Keep pinching yourself, Roy, it can be a dream come true.

As ever,

Del

An interesting letter from Del Schrader to the author regarding the upcoming plans for the treasure hunt to Glorieta Pass, including a reference to our partner, John McFarland. Jesse James III had a most remarkable knowledge of information about many things.

The first treasure sign we discovered--an old tree purposely bent when it was quite small. Later I realized that it was bent towards where the treasure had been. John McFarland is shown here next to it with a hole he had dug looking for the treasure.

The old Pigeon Ranch House at Glorieta Pass near where the treasure was buried. It was built in 1848 along the Old Spanish Trail. It also served as a stagecoach stop for many years. The largest Civil War battle in the West was fought here.

A view looking southeast showing the deep dry wash. After the photo was taken, I discovered that the treasure had been buried on the far edge of it, but a recent flood had washed the treasure away.

Another treasure sign that I found—a large, "smiling" face carved on the side of a huge rock outcropping. It was very old and it was looking towards where the treasure had been buried.

Here is the author looking at some odd carvings on a rock that resemble the left side of a smiling face which is looking towards were the treasure had been buried.

Here is an overall view looking southward. The large tree on the right was the first of the three large trees. The other two trees and the treasure site were on the left side of the large dry wash here in the middle of the picture.

This is the author and John McFarlane next to the bent "hoot owl" tree that I discovered. It was the first clue to the treasure.

This is the huge rock outcropping not far from the bent tree where I found the hole that had been drilled along its bottom that pointed directly to the three large trees were the treasure had been buried. One of my detectors can be seen at the left side of the picture.

This is the huge rock outcropping showing the large stone face carved out near the top. It's also the rock that had the hole drilled near the base at a 45-degree angle that pointed to the three trees and the treasure location

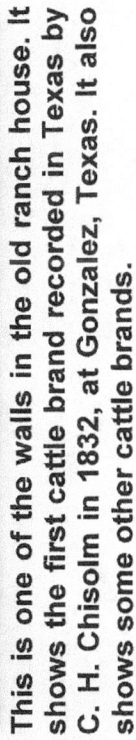

This is one of the walls in the old ranch house. It shows the first cattle brand recorded in Texas by C. H. Chisolm in 1832, at Gonzalez, Texas. It also shows some other cattle brands.

Here is the author looking at some odd carvings on a rock that resemble the left side of a smiling face which is looking towards were the treasure had been buried.

Here is an overall view looking southward. The large tree on the right was the first of the three large trees. The other two trees and the treasure site were on the left side of the large dry wash here in the middle of the picture.

This is the author with his VP-200 military mine detector and some of the battlefield relics he found.

This is one of the many handmade signs that had been put up around the area by the man who had lived there for many years and made a living by conducting tours. It was he who had found the treasure after a rainstorm uncovered it.

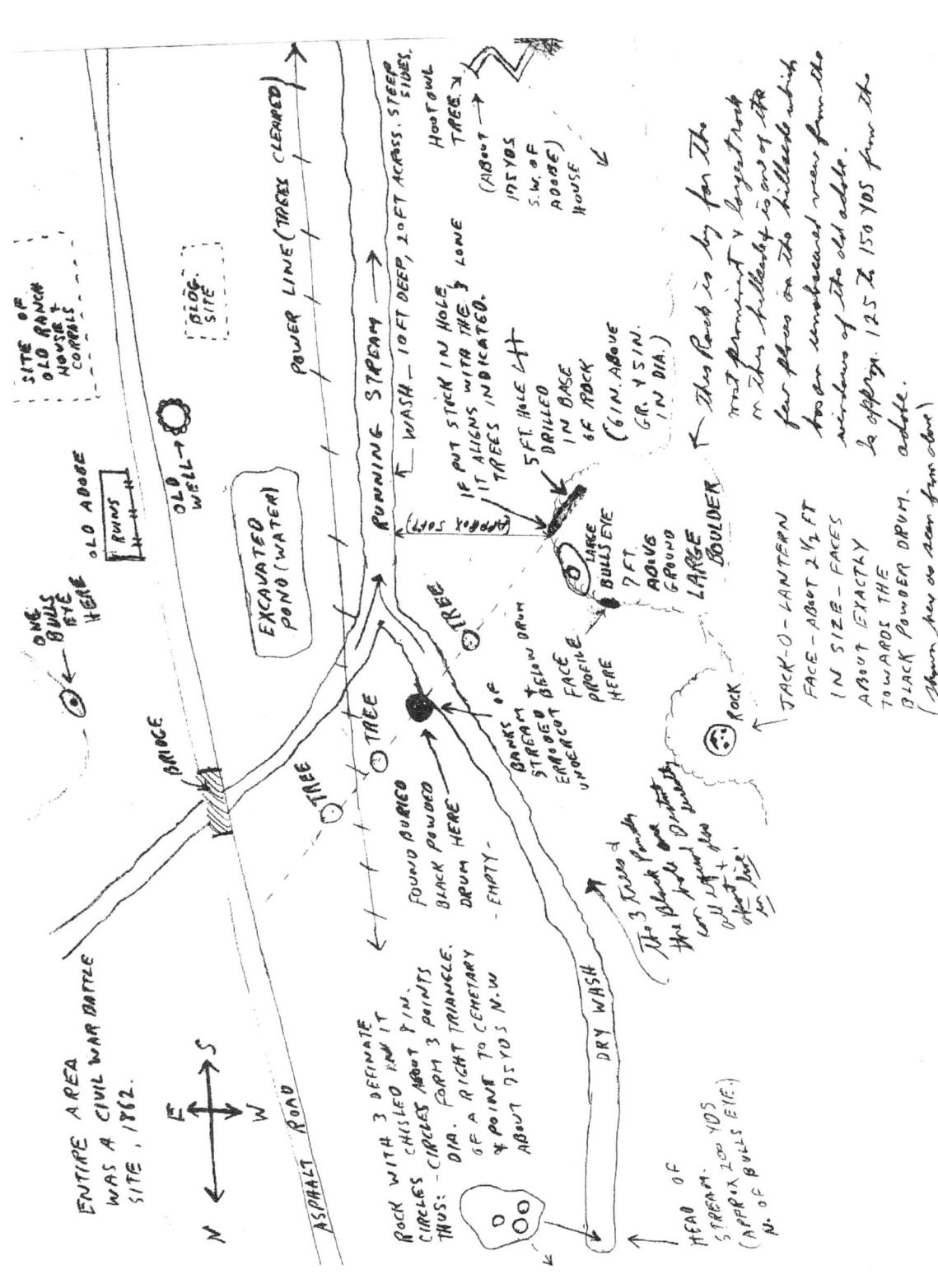

A crude map that I drew out when I got home showing the location of the treasure signs, the bent tree, the rock face, the 5-foot hole drilled into the face of the huge rock at a 45-degree angle that pointed to the three big trees that were perfectly aligned in the direction where the hole pointed, and the buried powder can directly over where the treasure had been on the edge of the dry wash.

Chapter Five

Del Writes a Book, *Jesse James Was One of His Names*

Within a week after we got home from Glorieta Pass, Del wrote up the story in the *Los Angeles Herald Examiner* Newspaper. Of course, we had met with Jesse James III and told him the bad news. But he was convinced that we had found where the treasurer had been. Although he added that Jesse James and some others had buried guns and other items under an old wagon wheel that should still be there, but we never saw any old wagon wheels.

Then, Jesse James III approached Del to write a book about himself and about the history of the Knights of the Golden Circle, its beginnings, who many of its prominent members were, and the part that Jesse James had played in it under many assumed names--meaning of course, that he had not been killed by Bob Ford, but had lived to a ripe old age. Del saw that the folder was thick and agreed, then paid Jesse James III a sum of money (about $1,500 or maybe more) that Jesse James III had insisted on for the material. Jesse James III gave him the first installment and Del started writing.

But soon, they got into an argument over the rest of the material when Jesse James III tried to compromise Del by upping the price for the rest. Apparently, he was in the process of making arrangements with another journalist in Central California to do the book instead. Del found out that Jesse James III had been pulling this stunt before with other writers, keeping the money, then finding another writer to repeat the process with. So, if Del had finished the book, Jesse James III could not pull the stunt again. However, Del was a professional journalist and was not so easy to be cheated. A violent argument finally ensued which ended when Jesse James III pulled a revolver on Del and threatened to kill him. That scared Del off.

Now, Del was stuck with a partial manuscript, plus being out a considerable amount of money. He also had made a deal with a book publisher for the book. We talked about the book and how Del could get the material to finish it up. Jesse James III was still being obstinate and uncooperative. It was plain that he did not want Del to finish the book. Then to my surprise, one day, Del began writing on the book again, which he entitled *JESSE JAMES WAS ONE OF HIS NAMES*. In a short time, the book was finished.

I was surprised and asked him how he had done that since he only had enough material for the first few chapters.

"Well, it just sorter came to me from what I had heard Jesse James III talk about."

There's no doubt that Del was a word merchant and it served him well in this case. The book was soon published but sales of it were poor. A lot of people found the story line too hard to believe. It's true that it did stretch credibility, especially since a large part of it dealt with Jesse James not being killed by Bob Ford, but instead, while using a number of assumed names, became an important member of the Knights of the Golden Circle and lived to a ripe old age while stealing or diverting huge sums of money to add to the huge treasure of the KGC to help finance their plans for a second Civil War.

The publisher soon pulled the book from the shelves and Del ended up with the rest, selling a few copies to his friends. He made me a gift of an autographed copy that I still have to this day. A couple of years after that, Del died suddenly of a heart attack and the family began dumping the books. Then for some reason, collectors and treasure hunters started buying up the books and the price escalated. The last I knew, they were selling for $100 or more with very few available.

Well, it was great armchair reading to say the least, but some historians and treasure hunters have a very high regard for the book and consider it as the "Bible" on its subject matter. I only wish that Del had lived long enough to see that happen.

Treasure Hunters' Trials

No Gold Here, But A Wealth Of History

By DEL SCHRADER
Herald-Examiner Staff Writer

"It was embarrassing to find ourselves fighting side by side with the damnyankees against the Apaches, but reassuring under the circumstances . . . the Yankees are sturdy fighters and will be tough to beat."

Thus did Capt. John James describe the little-known aftermath of the bloody, but indecisive Civil War Battle of Glorieta Pass, N.M., March 26-28, 1862, in a letter to his youngest brother, Jesse Woodson James, who would be later outlawed.

For three days, Apache Indians had watched the Union and Confederate soldiers slug it out at Valverde, Apache Canyon, Pigeon's Ranch and Johnson's Ranch about 16 miles southeast of Santa Fe. Confederate Gen. H.H. Sibley left Ft. Bliss in El Paso, Tex., with 3,800 men and returned with only 1,200.

When they considered the time opportune, the Apaches struck in a pincher movement from each end of the canyon and the soldiers in Blue and Gray closed ranks to fight off the determined Indian charges. When the Apaches were beaten off, the Civil War in New Mexico resumed.

Before Union Maj. John Chivington destroyed Rebel ammunition and supply wagons at Johnson's Ranch, Captain James and an aide grabbed a payroll chest containing $125,000 in $20 gold pieces, hauled it through the woods and buried it on Pigeon's Ranch.

In 1879, Jesse James, by this time an outlaw, bought 5,000 acres for $5,000 in Glorieta Pass to block tycoon Jay Gould from building the Santa Fe Railroad from Raton Pass to Santa Fe. Jesse was interested in furthering his Denver & Rio Grande (Chili Line) from Santa Fe to Alamosa, Colo., but he later sold Glorieta spur rights to Gould for $1 million, turning a nice profit.

James retained the Pigeon Ranch and in 1879 he and members of the Knights of the Golden Circle reburied the Confederate coin cache which would be worth about $1.5 million at today's prices. The ranch was sold to the Greer family in the early 1900s. It is currently leased by Bill Mahan, who manufactures the D-TEX treasure-finding devices in Graland, Tex.

Recently, Mahan gave permission to Roy W. Roush, Los Angeles treasure and artifact hunter, and two of his friends, Jack McFarland and Andy Miller, to "browse around" the 640-acre ranch.

The trio, armed with a Confederate map and a trunkful of electronic gear, found scores of minie balls, musket slugs, grape shot balls, pieces of cannon balls and other Civil War artifacts, but no gold coins.

Miller told The Herald-Examiner, "About five years ago a big flash flood washed out the springhead and created a miniature Grand Canyon. Using triangulations off our map, we found a Union Army black powder keg which marked the spot above the treasure chest and then we found an indentation of the chest in the wall — but somebody had already made off with it."

Roush added, "We discovered the modern power line right-of-way had destroyed some of the old Confederate signs and symbols, but we did find a number of clues: Jesse James' old Jack-o'-Lantern rock, the Silhouette Face, a Hoot Owl tree, a Golden Circle marker, the drilled directional hole, the old graveyard-cottonwood trees triangulation and, of course, the powder keg marker. They all pointed to the place where the chest was. Notice I said was."

McFarland volunteered, "It's too bad the state of New Mexico hasn't preserved the old Pigeon Ranch. Only the old adobe ranch house, started in 1848, remains. There's a lot of history up there."

Indeed there is. If the old ranch house could talk it would be a tale in itself. During the years Jesse W. James owned the house the following figures slept under its roof: Sen. William A. Clark, D-Mont.; Sen. Stephen B. Elkins, R-W. Va.; Sen. Henry Gassaway Davis, D-W.Va.; "Brushy Bill" Roberts (Billy the Kid); John Patterson (Jefferson Davis), the Sundance Kid, Butch Cassidy, Bob Dalton, Pancho Villa, Dr. Frank James, Kit Carson, Wyatt Earp, Morgan James and El Fago Baca.

Alternate Highway 84-85 now cuts the ranch in half. In the early days, freight wagons traveled the Santa Fe Trail from Independence, Mo., to Santa Fe and ultimately on to El Monte, Calif. Later came stagecoaches but the old stage station, barn, corrals and outbuildings have been torn down. Only the old house remains and its years are numbered because of neglect and vandalism. Across the road from the house is the 420-year-old Spanish well full of debris.

Signal Point, situated above the old house, has been used for a thousand years as a lookout. Centuries ago, Apaches and Navajos camped there en route to enslave peaceful Pueblo Indians.

In 1540, the Spaniard Coronado and his soldiers in search of the Seven Golden Cities of Cibola struggled across Pigeon Ranch. Indian marksmen, crouched on Signal Point, killed several of Coronado's men with their arrows. It was a hot day and the 7,400-foot altitude had caused the panting and frustrated soldiers to remove their helmets, thus sacrificing safety for comfort.

In 1699, Spanish Cap.-Gen. Diego De Vargas fought a series of skirmishes with Apaches dug in atop Signal Point. In 1846, during the early days of the Mexican War, Spanish Gov. Manuel Armijo made a half-hearted stand on Pigeon Ranch against U.S. Gen. Stephen Watts Kearney before falling back to Santa Fe and surrendering the city.

And in 1862 the Union and Confederate forces battled on the ranch. What were the Confederates doing at Santa Fe in the first place? Although Washington never acknowledged it, Texas claimed all land north and east of the Rio Grande River and Santa Fe, the present capital of New Mexico, was located east of the river so the Texans reasoned it was part of the Lone Star State.

Andy Miller, looking back on the days spent on the Pigeon Ranch, declared, "There's hardly a square foot that hasn't been dug up around the old ranch buildings. Even old Union and Confederate makeshift tombstones have been desecrated. I can't believe that Americans by nature are thieves and plunderers, but people who have illegally dug these holes, some of them big enough to bury a car in, destroyed a lot of history in their mad dash to uncover treasure.

"Gold-seekers, striking out wildly with the spades after their electronic gear has perhaps picked up a piece of tinfoil, generally are rewarded only with blisters, mosquito bites and frustration. In the meantime, historic treasures, far more valuable then gold, are wantonly destroyed."

"There are scientifically accepted ways to hunt for treasure. Use good equipment. Roy Roush had good luck finding artifacts with his VP-200, a modified Vietnam mine detector. Maps help as does information contained in letters written by Great Uncle John or some other ancestor. Terrain and soil should be studied. The size of underground roots give clues. Sometimes it pays to sit down, relax and ask yourself, 'Now if I was going to bury something valuable 75 or a 100 years ago where would I have buried it?' "

"A little common sense can pay dividends. Never, never move in on private or government property without permission and start digging enormous holes. If you do dig, cover up the holes before leaving. An experienced treasure hunter won't dig in a covered-up hole because he will notice the soil has been disturbed."

Jack McFarland grinned: "Hindsight is always better than foresight — but don't dig or go looking for a treasure that somebody removed five years before."

Angeleno Roy W. Roush displays pieces of Union cannonball picked up by his metal detector on Pigeon Ranch.

A Los Angeles Herald-Examiner, Sunday, September 16, 1973 A-9

Old Pigeon Ranch House
Seen from Signal Point where Indians stood in 1540 to shoot arrows at
Coronado's soldiers coming down road.

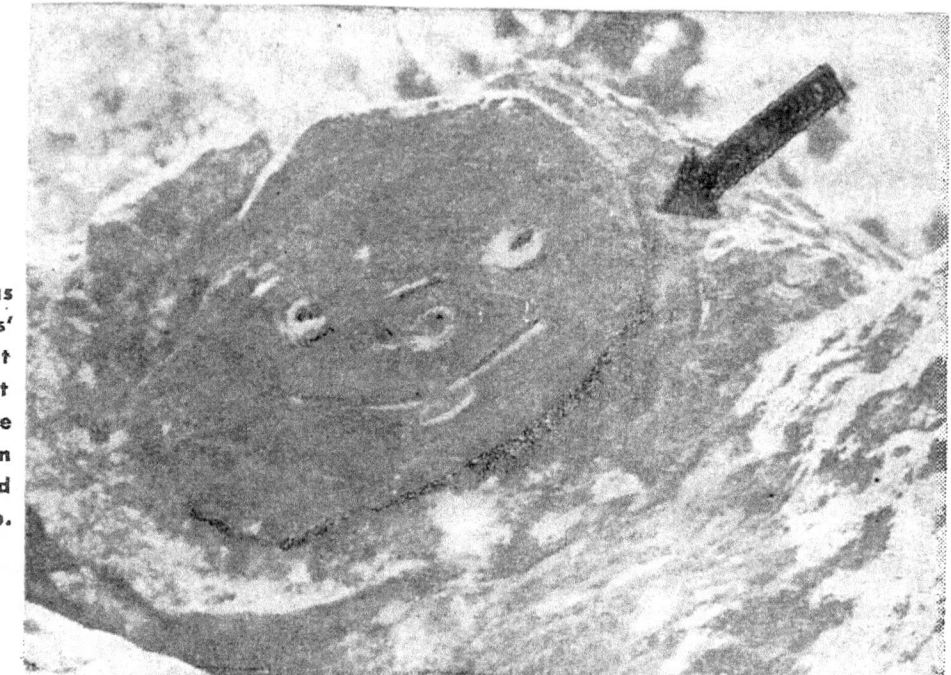

Round stone face was dubbed Jesse James' Jack-o'-Lantern. It helped locate buried loot which Angeleno treasure hunters found had been discovered and removed about five years ago.

Assorted artifacts from 1862 Civil War battle include grape shot, Confederate minie balls, musket slugs, cannonball pieces and horseshoes.

Roy Roush watches Jack Farland dig for a buried clue on side of a 7,400-foot peak on Pigeon Ranch, N.M.

The Race for $150 Billion In Buried Confederate Gold

Caches Located Everywhere, Pages 6 & 7

There's $150 Billion In Confederate Gold Buried In U.S. Just Waiting to Be Dug Up

Vast fortunes in gold now worth an estimated $150 billion were buried by die-hard Confederates and their supporters throughout North America in the 50 years following the Civil War.

And now that owning gold is legal for Americans, and selling it is more lucrative than ever, interest in the lost Rebel hoards has risen to a fever pitch.

A story that has existed since 1865 as tantalizing bits and pieces of legends and rumors, is erupting into a gold rush.

And old timers and treasure experts familiar with the Confederate Underground have an incredible tale to tell – of war heroes turned outlaws, thefts of epic proportions, booby-trapped treasure troves, and a secrecy pact the Mafia would envy. The most astonishing part is the amount that remains buried.

"Only a miniscule amount of the buried bullion has been found, primarily, I believe, because there's not a great flood of people searching for it," said Del Schrader, 54, a treasure hunter and newsman from Los Angeles.

"Undoubtedly there is the usual cynicism – people don't believe there's all that bullion laying around."

Besides, he added, the federal government until 1974 banned private ownership of gold and legislated the metal's price at a low $35 an ounce. But, more importantly, the men who amassed the fortune hid it well.

CALLING THEMSELVES the Knights of the Golden Circle, high-level Confederates joined together to beg, borrow and steal gold to finance a second try. The organization closed its books in 1916, but its oath of loyalty was kept by sons and grandsons into the 1970s.

Some elderly men, claiming to be descendents of Golden Knights members, said the secret group sprang into action almost immediately after Gen. Robert E. Lee surrendered.

By VAUN WILMOTT
Of the Tattler Staff

The Inner Sanctum, its leadership, reportedly included 12 famous and infamous Rebel veterans, Gen. William C. Quantrill (erroneously reported dead in a Union hospital in 1865), Col. Jesse James (the outlaw), John Patterson (Jefferson Davis' alias), Gen. Nathan B. Forrest (the brilliant cavalry leader), Gen. Bud Dalton, Lewis Dalton, George Payne, Prof. B.E. Bedeczek, George Baxter, Cole Younger, Gen. J.O. Shelby and Jack (Brac) Miller.

Their goal was to fight a Civil War replay, if it came, on a cash and carry basis without need to depend on profit-hungry international bankers.

The Golden Circle, headquartered in Nashville, Tenn., started with $7 billion in gold from the Confederacy's treasury, the oldtimers told Schrader. Its well-hidden coffers swelled as Southern veterans reaped post war fortunes by legal and illegal means.

The Confederate Underground supposedly infiltrated gold mines around the world, embezzling or stealing huge amounts to be smuggled back to the U.S. Some $32 million came from Afrikaners, the losers in Britain's Boer War, and an equal figure was pilfered from robber baron Jay Gould.

THERE ARE EVEN rumors that the group received some of the $50 billion in gold that a few experts claim has "disappeared" from Fort Knox over the years.

And every late-show fan knows how Rebel vets Jesse James, Cole Younger and the Daltons came into their wealth.

Confederate veterans profiting within the law also contributed — up to 50 per cent of their annual income, the story goes.

At any rate, contributions stopped flooding in in 1916, when the group officially disbanded. Inflation and the rising price of gold have done the rest.

According to one of the claimed Golden Circle descendents, Rebel treasure troves exist in almost every state and most Canadian provinces, plus $63 million in the Canary Islands. The caches include $500 million in the Dakotas, $630 million in New Mexico, $330,000 each in Nevada and Utah, $175 million each in Arizona and Washington, $333 million in New England and an even billion in Canada.

An obvious question is: "Why is it still there?"

FOR ONE THING, the Knights swore themselves and their descendents to secrecy. "It was almost a religious thing with them. Anyone who revealed the secrets of the Circle would have ended up dead," Schrader said.

Also, the men who hid the treasures guarded them with sophisticated, weatherproofed explosive booby-traps. More than one amateur has ended his treasure hunting career by tinkering with a Rebel cache, the old timers claim.

Many of the locations were memorized and never committed to paper — and eventually lost due to death and failing memories.

The terrain has changed in many places. A landslide in San Garbiel canyon buried a $1.6 million stash under 90 feet of rubble, one descendent said.

Furthermore, the Golden Circle Code forbade opening any deposit before the last Confederate veteran died. And by then federal laws had made private ownership of gold illegal and unprofitable.

The new gold ownership law changed things, of course. And the old timers, now between 68 and 92 years old, decided to make a few tantalizing details public.

SCHRADER, ACCOMPANIED by treasure expert Roy W. Roush, searched a remote New Mexico site for one cache. But since such famous outlaws as Butch Cassidy, the Sundance Kid, Jesse James and Billy the Kid were alleged to have stopped there, the place had already attracted scores of treasure hunters.

"That was the closest we ever got to a cache, in Glorieta Pass in New Mexico," Schrader said. "That's about 17 miles east of Santa Fe.

"We'd done a lot of investigative work and discovered the clues. This was the site of the largest Civil War battle in the West and we believed an army payroll had been buried there.

"We started work there and found the clues — like a hole in a boulder. If you stuck a long branch in that hole, it pointed in a certain direction. Then we found three trees close together, an unusually shaped branch on a tree and a jack-o-lantern face carved on a rock," he continued.

"A few more things led us to a spot and we started digging. We found an old black powder can which marked the spot above the treasure and we found the mark of a chest in the ground.

"But somebody had beaten us to it. Apparently, years ago there'd been tremendous rains which washed the earth away from the treasure. Local stories — or hints, anyway — were that somebody had found the gold and walked off with it."

ROUSH ADMITTED that he and Schrader are now working on another site. He narrowed the location down to "outside California."

"I believe we're just about the only ones actively seeking the Confederate bullion and we're working on this one cache – it's not in California – which we hope to locate this summer. Perhaps in July.

"We've gone to three different sources for our information and they've all checked out and confirm each other," he said.

"We believe this particular hoard has about $11 million in silver, $20 million in gold and $11 million in copper. We're working on putting together a big expedition on this one."

Charles Kenworthy, the scientific treasure hunter described in the May 18 TATTLER, is reportedly working with his Stanford Research Institute cohorts on one huge cache. The federal government has granted his team permission to search one of its military reservations.

LIKE KENWORTHY, Schrader and Roush are reluctant to reveal details about hidden treasure, although they claim to know the general locations of many caches.

"For example, there's about $200 million in gold buried under a freeway near Sacramento," Schrader said. **"And about 11 miles from Nashville, there's a repository of $4 billion."**

Both men claim to have interviewed descendents of Golden Circle members and studied the old records thoroughly. They warn against underestimating the skill of the men who hid the treasures.

"THEY USED THE very best engineers they could find when that bullion was hidden," Schrader said. "And they used the finest materials in hiding the treasure and also protecting it with booby-traps.

"And make no mistake about it – those booby-traps are still operative. Don't think the powder's wet or the trigger mechanism has decayed. It hasn't, and those caches are deadly to anyone who doesn't know what he's doing."

DEL SCHRADER (right) and Roy Roush examine treasure maps.

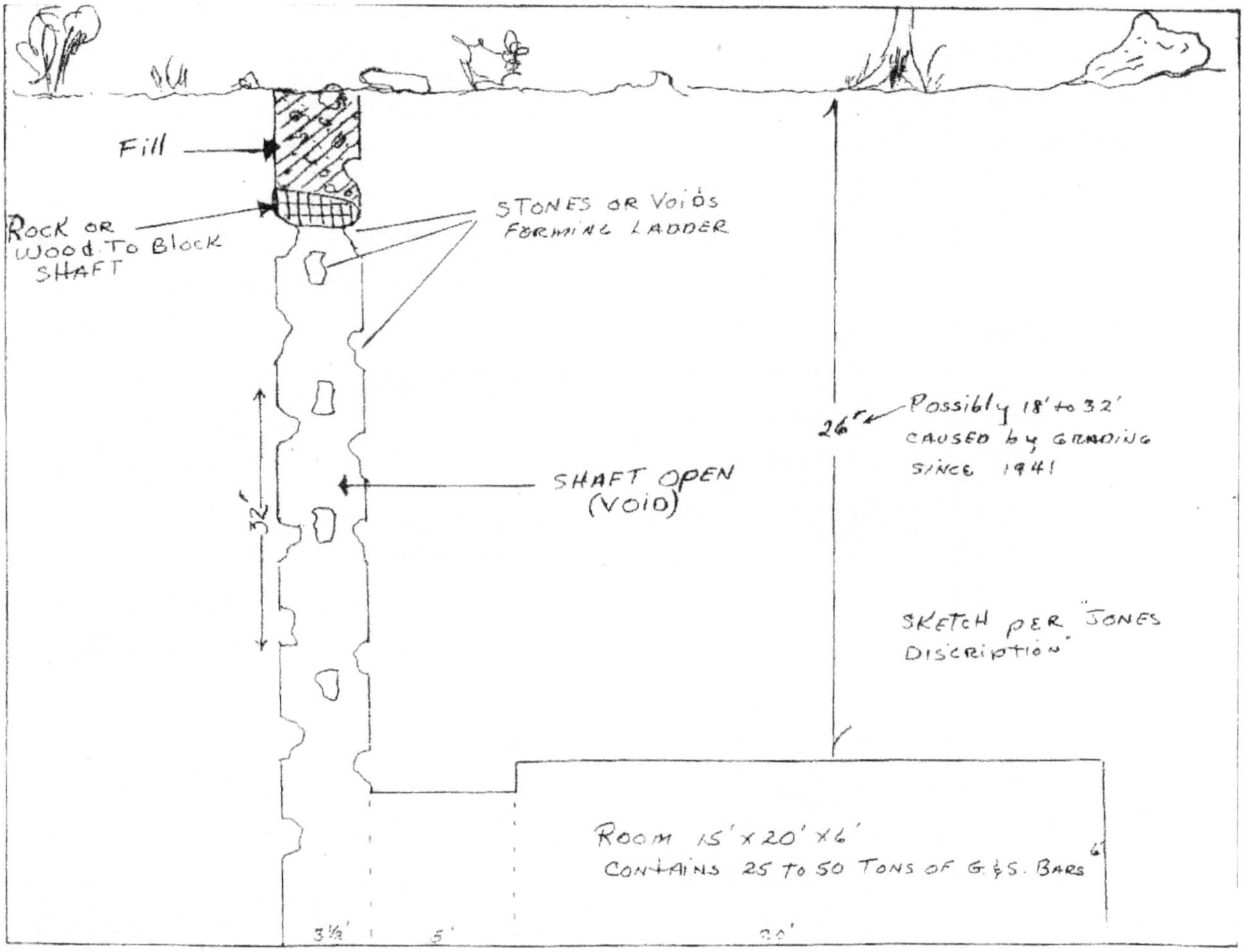

Sketch labels:
- Fill
- Rock or Wood to Block Shaft
- Stones or Voids Forming Ladder
- Shaft Open (Void)
- 32'
- 26' — Possibly 18' to 32' caused by grading since 1941
- Sketch per Jones Discription
- Room 15' x 20' x 6' contains 25 to 50 tons of G & S. Bars
- 3½' , 5'

DRAWING shows how Confederate troops buried their gold after the war, hoping eventually to dig it up and renew the war between the states. Many similar underground gold cache's are located throughout North America, experts say.

ODD SHAPED tree branch and 'jack-o-lantern rock (left) were discovered by Roush after following clues gathered from information supplied by old-timers and descendents of Rebel Golden Knights members. Roush found proof a chest at one time had been buried at the site.

Our partner, John McFarland, examines our first treasure clue, a badly deformed old tree made that way by the KGC. It is known as a "Hoot Owl" tree. They were one of the most commonly used treasure signs used by the KGC to mark where they had buried treasure (sometimes three together.)

(THE) STAR
NEW YORK, N.Y.
DEC 23 1975

Hunt is on for $150 billion rebel hoard

By VAUN WILMOTT

THE HUNT is on for a $150 billion fortune buried in secret hideouts across the U.S. and Canada and guarded by deadly booby traps.

The treasure is the lost Rebel's Hoard, and it was buried more than 60 years ago by a secret Confederate society planning a second Civil War.

Now two veteran treasure hunters who have been tracking down the fortune in gold and silver bullion say they're on the verge of a major discovery.

Del Schrader and Roy Roush of Los Angeles say the find is "near California" and that it contains $20 million in gold, $11 million in silver and $11 million in copper.

"We've gone to three different sources for our information and they've all checked out and confirmed each other," says Roush.

The treasure was hidden by the secret Southern society Knights of the Golden Circle, who were sworn not to reveal its location under pain of death. They didn't trust maps, so they memorized everything.

The Knights disbanded in 1916, and by then the fortune was scattered throughout North America.

Some of it has been lost forever: A $1.6 million hoard in the San Gabriel Mountains was buried under 90 feet of rubble in a landslide, and a freeway was built over $200 million in Sacramento, Calif.

Schrader and Roush have interviewed many of the descendants of the Golden Knights and examined thousands of ancient documents. They've also used psychics, engineers, museums and newspaper files in their search.

The closest they've gotten to a cache was near Glorieta Pass in New Mexico—about 17 miles east of Santa Fe. But heavy rains had washed away the treasure.

But Schrader says the main reason so little has been found was because the Knights knew exactly what they were doing.

"It was almost a religious thing with them," he told The Star. "Anyone who revealed their secrets would have ended up dead. And the survivors, now aged between 68 and 92, have poor memories."

The Knights also forbade the opening of any hoard until the last survivors died. Only now are fragments of information dribbling out.

"And don't forget those boobytraps—they've already killed and wounded a few unsuspecting treasure hunters," said Roush. "Those caches are deadly to anyone who doesn't know what he's doing."

Here are the known locations of some of the treasure: $500 million in the Dakotas, $630 million in New Mexico, $175 million in Arizona and Washington, $333 million in New England, $4 billion near Nashville, Ten., $330,000 each in Nevada and Utah, $1 billion in Canada and $63 million in the Canary Islands.

1011 East Ninth Street,
Beaumont, California 92223,
September 30th, 1973.

Mr. Roy Roush,
425 North Sycamore Ave., #5,
Los Angeles, California 90036

Dear Roy:

Just a line to let you and John Del., etal know that with those terrible teeth out, at long last I now have those automatic--chompers installed, I guess that in time they will become smoother, etc etc. Man alive, I am grateful indeed. How I wished that I had-had everything set and this all over and done with so I could have gone to Gloriets and looked myself. There is another bigger cache near, but having the inside track, knowing what to expect and to do there,

I have in my mind, since winter will hit Montana sooner this fall, of an Indian gathering place in Oklahoma, several small treasures and near another one which is worth about $75,000,000.00, more or less at to-day's values, which isnt beans nor corn cobs. But, again** we are not going to tackle it with out proper backing, I think, I can buy a small tract, get about three treasures out on the river, then move over just a few miles and get busy on the big treasure probaly about 12 to 16 feet deep, since some erosion took place and more dirt was dropped by a floded condition upon the treasure stated location, but this will take my time and my know-how, with your experience and your help......

Grand-dad sold out a railroad ownership to a multi-millionaire some years ago, the purchaser bought the rail road for a son, an only son. Grand-dad took $6,000,000,00, more or less, and placed it in a bank, he took as said $14,000,000.00, more or less, telling me he buried it along the old railway system just off, down and under solid rock also in Texas, it will take your maganatometer, and a plane fying up and down the old railraod until we hit a sign and possible exact spot. That one

At present day values this treasure should also be worth, in my own humble opinion another estimated $75,000,000.00, more or less. Now this I can do, this I can lead out on. Also the Jefferson Davis treasure in east of Dallas, or east of where Old Cyenne, once stood. Then that is in three huge steel chests in a swampy place, down and under water.

Near there, in the near vacinity is a hollow log pipe line, hewn out of cypress logs, a water line runs for around 20 miles, from a big spring to a certain commercial facility was pumped water for the factory's needs.

Along about every third and some times every fifth hollow cypresswood pipe is buried a treasure. You will eventually find that The JwJ organization used certain formulas for burying treasures with which they would have been ready to dig up in case of C I V I L W A R II, they buried treasures and made measurements in multiples of 3's, 5's 6's., then on another system went into using multiples of 4's, 5's, and 11's.

Letters from Jesse James III

One must remember that when King Solomon built the great Masonic Temple, there was no provisions made for a north door, also remember that the WORSHIPFUL MASTER sits in the EAST, while the SENIOR WARDEN sits in the WEST. Truely one of the most amazing systems ever devised by mortal man. Everything they did was done so silently, so secretly and so carefully that not the sound of a single hammer was ever heard. Everything was done so perfectly and so masterfully, that never a single secret ever leaked out openly, not once. Many masters benefitted, many fellows and brothers were taught worthy lessons, etc etc.

So, once again, I am ever so grateful to have gotten the BAD TEETH problem over with, now next is my heart specialist-examination, I feel great, but, I must admit, it was frustrating and a terrible let-down not to receive not even one thin dime advanced royalty after so many long wmonths, and years of too many sacrifices to be mentioned, then not even get a thing by which I could have paid off my full dental bill.

Like I said, thus far Del as is, has barely touched the surface and I haven't even begun to open up on Confederate secrets etc etc. It has been said many times, that Grand-dad JwJ used the Bible, 'let not thy right hand know what thy left hand doeth.' It was also said that NO MAN EVER KNEW ALL OF JwJ's business nor activities, not even Uncle COLE, not even Uncle Dr Frank James, not even my dad, my dad's twin brother, not any of my Uncles, Aunts either. But, in the years of close associations with Grand-dad JwJ, he told me perhaps almost the whole and entire story and activities. Now, I am the last man alive who can and who will, GOD WILLING, get busy at last. But, if I am to continue and continue to repeatedly be the patsy, I wont be around nor alive to show any man much more, nor indicate further facts. I saw kinsleen making the self same errors while JwJ was alive, offering to clear matters up, it proved as usual that I was the one and only one on the ball nor ready at all times to go set some of my dear cousins up for life with GOLD etc etc.

I told you guys the story of the SHERIFF, and CONSTABLE and myself, and what happened, if we go down there, this fact can be shown and proven by eye wittnesses if you knew where and with whom dependable facts can be brought from the darkeness to the light. Prsocrastination, lack of just plain guts, cost the three of us a flat $6,000,000.00, more or less, at that date, and probably would have been worth three times that much to-day. If that isnt one of the lessons, then I give up. Adios, JJ

Mr. Bill ███████,
Box ████
Roanoke, Va. 24014

1011 East Ninth Street,
Beaumont, California 92223,
February 20th., 1974

Dear Bill:

Tanks for your good letter mailed on February 14th., last. I will hasten to reply to your well put questions. While I get some of my mail 6 miles east of here at anning, I do so as sort of a buffer, and for obvious reasons, just in ease, if you know what I mean?????

Here is the pitcube, eight years ago, or maybe nine years past, I had a lot of disruptions and troubles. So, I pulled up stakes and took off from Texas to Georgia, Alabama, Mississippi, Arkansas, hence on west to Arizona, back to Texas and Oklahoma, hauling a huge U-Haul Trailer loaded with priceless documents and records and personal data of my own family. I wont go into the why, but, I had no home anymore, so I unloaded at different towns some of the belongings, to relieve the terrible ordeal and stored many items in Arizona, Oklahoma, Colorado, Texas, Missouri Kansas, etc etc. While I have rounded up some and have it packed again ready for another change of residence, I still have a lot of very important items in storage, one place I owe a balanace now of $1550.00, and in Missouri around $1300.00, $500.00 in Oklahoma, and a slim balance now of $350.00 in Dallas area, Texas. I have been paying best I c an when I can.

I have tens upon tens of tens of thousands of dollars invested plus over 50 years now, and that is, indeed something, isnt it? Right now I am all packed-up to shove off for Texas via Utah, as we used to live in Utah and Colorado, as well as Myoming and also Montana, doing a lot of commutting back and forth etc etc. I would have to un-pack a lot of data and scrap books, documents etc etc, plus hundreds of photographs and negatives, and that would run my wife wilder than she is. We have been married for seven years this coming May-1974. She is a couple years older than I am, and her whole family and herself knew Grand-dad Jesse Woodson ames very-very well, and me too, as a kid tagging along behind Grand-dad.

About the book, I colaborated with a well known reporter of Los Angelese. He was a skeptic at first, but soon saw and realized that his own grand-dad etal on both sides his family were deeply loyal to and deeply involved with our folks over many-many years. So, he got busy, wrote the book,

The old men, members of KNIGHTS of the GOLDEN CIRCLE etc etc., trained me for years, everything, like the work in the Masonic Lodge is taught by word of mouth. I am, no doubt the LAST MAN, I am THE MAN FROM HEADQUARTERS! Roscoe James, R. E. James, Smith James, and many of out group are now dead, just a few remain alive to-day. All around you, ery where you look are openings for your pleasure, once you get the right approach. If I was down there, as everywhere else, I would soon have things organized and information pouring into my records. But, I cant teach you in a few hours that which took me a life time to absorb. And, I dont know to what church you belong, it does make a difference, once yo see the inner side of the once powerful organization, more than once.

Like the old Negro said, "Shucks, youall aint seen nuttin yet."

Kindest regards, I am

Yours sincerely,

Jesse James III

Mr. Del Schrader
Los Angeles Herald-Examiner
Los Angeles, California

P.O. Box ▮▮▮
Roanoke, Va. 24014
March 4, 1974

Dear Mr. Schrader:

I am writing you concerning my research interest in Mr. Jesse James III of Banning, California. After reading your series of articles in the Herald-Examiner two years ago, I wrote to Jesse and have been corresponding with him since that time. I am now in the last several months of preparing a manuscript on the American Civil War which will be published by Western Islands of Belmont, Massachusetts. My interest in Jesse developed from his statements about the Knights of the Golden Circle. He seemed to be very much in line with what my information and research on the K.G.C. indicated. The thesis of my book is to demonstrate the role of the K.G.C. and the organizations which were its roots in precipitating the nationwide filibustering and secession movements that brought on the war. Also, their involvement behind Lincoln's assassination. My research had indicated that the post-1869 and post-1915 Ku Klux Klans were to some extent continuations of the K.G.C. Jesse's claims seemed to be in accord with this.

Anyway, for two years I have been trying to make clear to Jesse that a historian like myself cannot use his story or any portion of it without seeing his evidence. After many letters from him (as you are probably quite familiar) full of interesting, but confusingly disorganized, unsupported claims, I have concluded that I will not be able to see any evidence he may have before my book's deadline is here. Jesse told me that a L.A. journalist had prepared and was ready to publish his full story.* I assume he meant you. Can you tell me if this is so, when it will be published so I can get a copy? If it is being delayed beyond this month, would it be possible for me to pay to borrow or purchase Xerox copies of those portions of the manuscript which discuss the K.G.C., Jesse James' relation to it, the K.G.C. after the war and the gold they buried in preparation for a second war, and the plans for same. I am not interested in the portions strictly on James and his associates unrelated to the K.G.C. and the Civil War. Any information you can provide me on this will be appreciated, fully acknowledged in my book, and I will provide any costs necessary for copying, postage, etc. Thank you very much. Telephone number, call collect: 703-344-1250.

Sincerely,

Bill ▮▮▮
Bill ▮▮▮

*P.S. I am enclosing a copy of a letter recently received from Jesse. I would appreciate any comments or light you may be able to cast on it.

Del Schrader

ARCADIA, CALIF. 91006

Mr. Bill ~~McIlhany~~:

March 14, 1974

I have marked your most unusual letter of March 4 as Exhibit No. 116 in a long line of harassment which has taken place since Jesse James III and I began assembling a book on his famous grandfather.

I don't know you from Adam, Mr. McIlhany, so consequently have learned to exert great caution in talking or writing to strangers. You profess to be an author so I find it hard to believe your most unusual request for parts of our manuscript which relate to the Knights of the Golden Circle. Our publisher has already purchased the hardcover rights and if you would stop to think to even consider your proposition would be most unethical on our part.

Morever, I resent you calling Mr. James confused, disorganized, unsupported, etc. He might use bad grammar or spell incorrectly at times, but he is one of the smartest men I've ever worked with.

In your postscript, you invite my comment on Jesse's letter of Feb. 20 to you. I have a completely legal financial and moral arrangement with Mr. James so no comment on my part is either necessary or prudent. I can only presume that Mr. James is "decoying" you. He spent 40 years at his grandfather's knee and certainly picked up some tricks from Jesse Woodson James, who had more charisma in his "nipped" left forefinger than J.F. Kennedy had in his entire body.

Early in the game, Mr. James told me, "I'm warning you, Del, there are people who don't want this book published." I soon knew what he meant. Odd "visitors" began popping up posing as something they weren't. I started getting anonymous letters and phone calls at work. I finally found it necessary to "bury" the research in numeous locations around the country to keep it from falling into the hands of the wrong people.

Our book will be published in the next month or so. Without being egotistical, I'm sure our book on Grandpa Jesse will render most Civil War books obsolete. I suggest you wait and read the book and the chapter on the K.G.C. It will amaze you--along with millions of readers around the world.

Your letter of March 4 had all the earmarks of a fishing expedition. In more than 30 years in the newspaper and TV writing business, I have yet to run into an "author" wanting to "borrow or purchase" Xerox copies of a script prior to it being published. You are either foolish, someone's tool or naive.

You cannot drive a wedge between Mr. James and myself. I've already run into some prize idiots who have tried. In a letter to our publisher, Mr. James wrote, "Del Schrader has succeeded where 100 other writers and/or authors failed." That's high praise from a man who worked 40 years so the world could know the truth about his grandfathe

Del Schrader

DEL SCHRADER

Chapter Six

A Treasure Hunters Convention in Tulsa and a Visit to KGC Territory

As I mentioned before, I had been a writer for a number of treasure magazines and publications since about 1966. Then in 1987, I joined the staff of the *Treasure Hunter Confidential Newsletter* as co-editor and part owner. This highly regarded monthly newsletter was by subscription only for $100 per year. It was considered the top publication on the subject for serious treasure hunters with lots of inside information including leads as to where treasurer might be found and I had written numerous stories about the treasures of the KGC. The other co-owner was Steve Ryland, well known in this field for many years and the owner of Cal-Gold, a gold prospecting and treasure hunting store in Pasadena, California. He had one of the sharpest technical minds I ever knew, and he was a great friend.

MY PROGRAM ON THE KGC AND THEIR TREASURES

Steve and I were invited to attend this annual meeting of The Federation of Metal Detector and Archaeology Clubs at Tulsa, Oklahoma in 1997 to make a special presentation on the treasures of the KGC. I posted the walls with dozens of articles on the KGC and their treasure trove. When I made the presentation at one o'clock, it was standing room only. I gave a short history of the organization and why they had buried huge amounts of treasure around the United States. Then, I showed slides of my recent trip to Glorieta Pass, New Mexico where I had discovered that the treasure had already been found. When we started running over-time, we adjourned to another room where most of the audience followed.

Public information on the KGC and their treasures was relatively new at that time. Most of the audience was amazed and asked Steve and I questions for hours. Eventually, a few from the audience began to join in offering bits of information they knew about. Among them was a gentleman that I had correspondence with before. His name was "Hillbilly" Bob Brewer from Mena, Arkansas. I was aware that he had knowledge on the subject, but for obvious reasons had mostly remained silent and had never sought publicity.

It was here that I learned some more on the subject. We all listened intently at what he related and his photographs and at some of the small items he had brought. Bob and been hunting for the KGC treasures for many years in southwestern Arkansas and also across the line into Oklahoma. A lot of that area was where Jesse and Frank James, along with their cousins, the Younger Brothers, had pulled off many robberies of banks, trains and stagecoaches. The money was rarely recovered and treasure hunters believe much of it was buried there to be added to the KGC treasure trove.

The long meeting was still going on when I retired to my room about 1:30 a.m. Even then, one person followed me to my room for more discussion. Hillbilly Bob had amazed us all with some very convincing evidence about the existence of the treasure and that it was spread over large areas of many states, especially in the southern states. He never directly said that he had recovered any of it, but you could draw your own conclusions.

A FIELD TRIP TO SOUTHWESTERN ARKANSAS

The next morning, Bob invited myself and two of my good treasure hunting friends, John Melancon and Bryan Hines to accompany him back to Mena, Arkansas where he promised that he would show us around some of the areas he had been talking about.

We eagerly took up his invitation. John and I had been good friends since we had met a few years before when I had been hired by a Japanese television film crew to organize a group to go to northwestern New Mexico to search for the well-known and famous "Seventeen Tons of Gold Bars." that had been buried there in 1930 by a group of wealthy Mexicans. They had secretly flown the gold in from Mexico in an old Ford Trimotor with the intent to sell it to the US Government for $30 an ounce. That was twice the amount they could get in Mexico. However, no sooner had they brought it into this country than President Roosevelt took the United States off of the gold standard. That made it illegal for anyone to possess more than one ounce of gold. Now, it was illegal contraband and they had to leave it where it was. Eventually, all of the Mexicans died and treasure hunters have been looking for it for years.

John had owned a treasure hunting shop at Aztec, New Mexico, a small town next to Farmington. He was extremely knowledgeable about the buried gold and he joined my 10-man team, along with some of his friends, making a very valuable contribution to the success of the film, even though we did not discover the treasure—though we would have been if it had been where we were searching.

We spent the first night at a motel in Mena. The next morning Hillbilly Bob came by to show us many items that he had picked up around the area, including numerous odd-shaped items made of iron that he had found with a detector--all clues to where KGC treasures were supposedly buried. The three of us were amazed. Then Bob took us to his favorite restaurant where I ordered a plate of biscuits and country gravy, the best I've ever had.

Following that, Hillbilly Bob loaded us into his four-wheel-drive vehicle to show us physical evidence of what the members of the KGC and left behind.

THE MYSTERIOUS TREASURE SIGNS

We traveled all day through very remote and heavily wooded areas to about four different locations. We got a very interesting education and were amazed at what we saw. It consisted mostly of curiously shaped rocks and trees that were bent or deformed. I'm sure that Hillbilly Bob had not put them there since they were far too old for that. The trees I would estimate to be about 100 years old and all the rocks had moss and lichen growing on them. Wherever we found deformed trees, there were always mysteriously shaped rocks near them, but not placed in any kind of arrangement or pattern that seemed to make any sense.

The rocks varied in size with the smallest and the most numerous (the diamond shaped ones) measuring from approximately six inches up to approximately two feet. The sides were very smooth and flat. Whoever made these had obviously spent a considerable amount of time to shape these rocks that perfectly. The other most numerous ones were shaped like a short boot, or perhaps more like an over-shoe. Those were mostly about actual size. But the strange thing is that they all had been very carefully made to a certain pattern, only the size varied. The arrangement of the diamond shaped rocks was very close to the Masonic Emblem, which has one end a little longer than the other.

The thickness of these rocks was always consistent with its length. The same pretty much held true for the boot-shaped rocks. Even though these rocks were obviously man-made, they were placed about in a manner that no one would particularly notice them or suspect what they were--unless you were especially looking for them. Then, you could see a pattern, but not enough that would lead you to solve the treasure location unless you were well versed on how to follow these signs. Perhaps some of these shaped rocks were also around the bent tree than I had discovered at Glorieta Pass, New Mexico a few years before, but not knowing then what I had just learned here, I probably didn't notice them, and that is exactly what had been intended.

Wherever we found the man-made rocks, there were always bent or deformed trees close by. And wherever we found bent or deformed trees, we found these rocks within sight. Again I would like to emphasize that to the uninitiated, or somebody just walking by, they probably wouldn't give more than a second glance to either the trees or the rocks and never guess at their significance. That is what the people wanted who put them. Notice, I said people, because what we saw in just a few hours would have taken considerably more than the full lifetime of any one individual, or several individuals Obviously, it had taken many people to create what we saw in just several areas. When considering what we observed represented only a very small portion of the areas around the country that had these shaped stones and bent trees, certainly hundreds of people must have been involved.

In fact, a few days later, I discovered some of these very same signs on an old farm hundreds of miles away in Kansas that my father had owned when I was a child in the 1930's. That story is coming up in the next chapter. So, I asked myself what was the purpose of these curiously shaped rocks and bent trees? If they were not treasure signs, then what could they possibly be? It must be taken into consideration that times were very hard following the Civil War, and people had a hard time making a living, so they did not have much time to spend away from their work just to bend a lot of trees and make a lot of carefully shaped rocks. There had to be a better reason!

I took a number of photographs, but only in certain areas and with the approval of Hillbilly Bob. These photos are included at the end of this chapter with descriptions of each. John, Brian and myself were astonished at the vast number of the bent trees and shaped rocks that we saw scattered over such a very large area. Hillbilly Bob carefully explained why some of the trees were shaped as they were, and also gave information on many of the rocks and what they meant. For example, he showed us validation marks on the bottom of some of the diamond-shaped rocks. This consisted of a corner being knocked off on the underside of the stone. Presently, I began to discover some of these rocks myself, some that Hillbilly Bob had not noticed before. One strange looking one that I found near a bent tree, Bob became particularly interested in. He identified it as a death sign, meaning that the treasure nearby was booby-trapped. He asked me to carefully place it back in position where I had found it since he was still working on that location.

ARMED KGC SENTINELS HAD PROTECTED THE TREASURES

He also showed us a false treasure hole at one location, purposely put there as a decoy to deceive any treasure hunters away from the actual treasure site. The explanation was that every few days, or maybe once a week, the appointed sentinel for that area would ride by and if he noticed any digging at the false treasure hole, he would set up an ambush to kill anyone if they returned. We noticed that someone had indeed, dug into the hole years ago. When we asked Hillbilly Bob about it, that's when he told us about the sentinels. Those guys really meant business and had sworn, under penalty of death, to protect the treasure and not to reveal any information regarding the locations of any treasure, nor to recover it themselves.

THE BIBLE TREE

In addition to the bent trees and the shaped rocks, Bob took us to one special location where the sides of an old Birch tree was full of old and mysterious carvings. He referred to it as the "Bible Tree" since it seemed to refer to parts of the Bible. Bob had spent years studying it and gave us an exclamation of what some of the markings meant. He highly regarded the tree as one of the most important signs left by the KGC.

Not surprisingly, he never showed us where any treasure was supposedly buried, nor did he ever tell us how close we might have been to one. That would have been giving away too much information to individuals like ourselves who were experienced treasure hunters.

The day I spent on that trip was one of the most memorable in my life and we were all three thoroughly convinced that what we had seen must have been treasure signs. It's true that we did not see the letters KGC nor the words "Knights" anywhere, but we did think it was significant that the most numerous of the shaped rocks were those in a diamond shape, which was like the emblem of the Masons, and many of the Masons were known to be members of the KGC.

Hillbilly Bob and I have kept in touch since then and have even shared my display table at some of the big treasure hunting shows held annually in Texas by the Texas Council of Treasure Hunting Clubs where he would display some of the latest items he had recovered in his search for treasure. They were not treasure itself, but were interesting things that had been planted as treasure clues. But so far, he has never admitted to actually making any finds, but I have wondered why he has never worked at a job for many years.

In 2002, he came to the show with a new book he had just published. It was entitled "Shadow of the Sentinel." It was a six-by-eight-inch hardback published by Simon and Schuster. It went into detail about a lot of his activities and covered much more than he had shown us or told us about, including how he had made a few recoveries. It is a fine book and most unique. I have an autographed copy and I recommend it to anyone interested in learning about the KGC, their signs, and their treasure. Perhaps though, Bob sees a lot more KGC treasure signs associated with various places and events than I do...however, he has found some of it, and so far, I've only found where some of it had been--but that may change soon!

Then, on the night of November 19, 2004, Bob was interviewed on NBC's "Nightline" with him telling some of his stories, plus some footage of him finding a few gold coins with a metal detector in southeastern

Oklahoma that he said he found by solving some of the clues that led to the treasure location.

Hillbilly Bob is still looking for more Knights of the Golden Circle treasures that have been buried around many parts of the United States…and most of it is still there waiting to be found!

The author giving a presentation on the Knights the Golden Circle and their treasures at a treasure hunter's convention in Tulsa, Oklahoma in 1997.

Two days after the convention, John Melanscon, Brian Hines and the author was taken to this very remote and heavily wooded area in southwestern Arkansas by "Hillbilly" Bob Brewer, where we were shown dozens of treasure signs supposed left by the Knights of the Golden Circle 100 years before. And though there's no proof, I have every reason to believe that they were genuine.

This was one of the most unusual looking deformed trees. It was rather grotesque.

A tree in the sign of a cross with a rather noticeable 30-degree bend above the cross. Is it leaning forwards or backwards? It also has bent trees around it.

Another deformed tree--possibly two trees that were grafted together.

Bob Brewer points out a clue carved on this old tree.

One of the most unusal man-shaped trees. It had three 90-degree turns and beneath it was a "Death Rock" meaning the treasure was booby trapped.

John Melancon is shown here taking a picture of "Hillbilly" Bob Brewer as he is explaining the bent trees and the odd man-made rocks in the area.

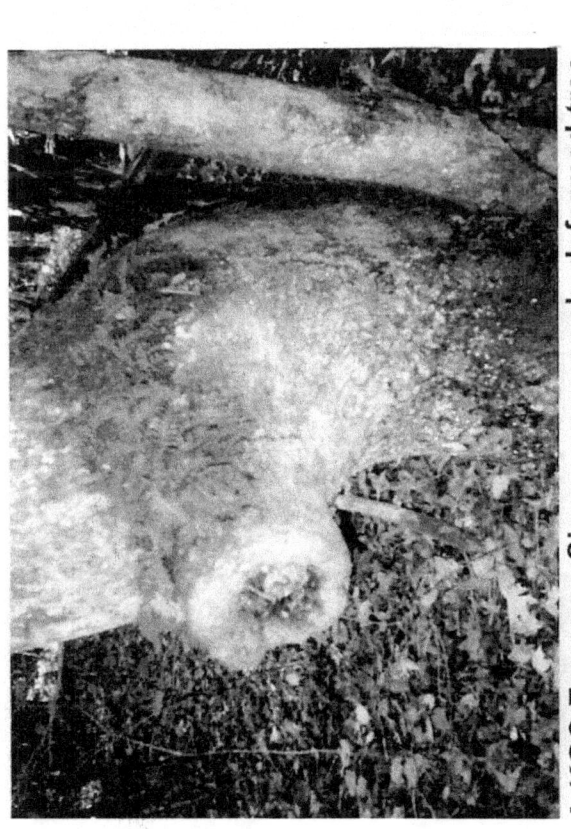

A KGC Treasure Sign—a purposely deformed tree that most people wouldn't even notice. And around all of these trees were man-make rocks.

One of the best examples of a purposely deformed tree. They would never grow like this on their own. It's at least 100 years old.

When a fallen tree blocked the road, it was no problem for Bob Brewer.

Another man-made stone with a different shape from most of the rest.

This is the old workshop where some of the odd shaped stones were made.

This is where Mel Fisher dug for KGC treasure. Rumors were that he did find some here.

116

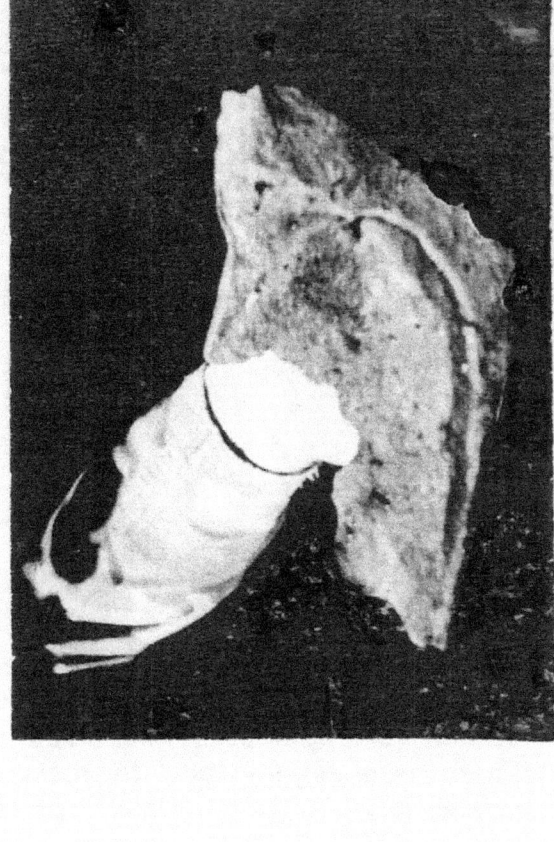

This is the "Death Rock" the author found beneath the tree with the three 90-degree turns. We placed it back in place exactly as it was.

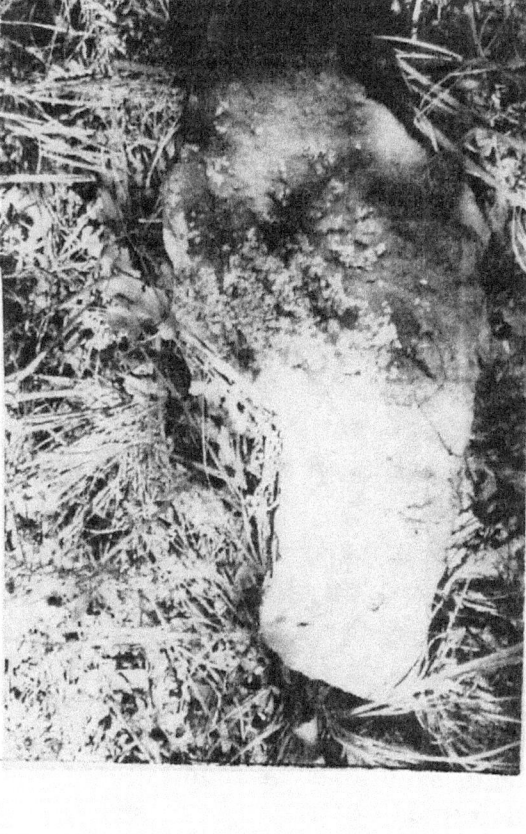

Another boot-shaped rock. All these peculiar man-made rocks had a special meaning to those who knew what they meant

Another example of a man-made rock.

This rock and been carved out to resemble a small boot. It was about 15-inches long. We saw several more like it near the bent trees.

A very large and heavy, man-made, diamond shaped rock almost 3 feet long lying exactly as we found it near one the deformed tree's.

The author is shown here holding another example of a man-made rock. There was significance to their size, arrangement, and direction they pointed.

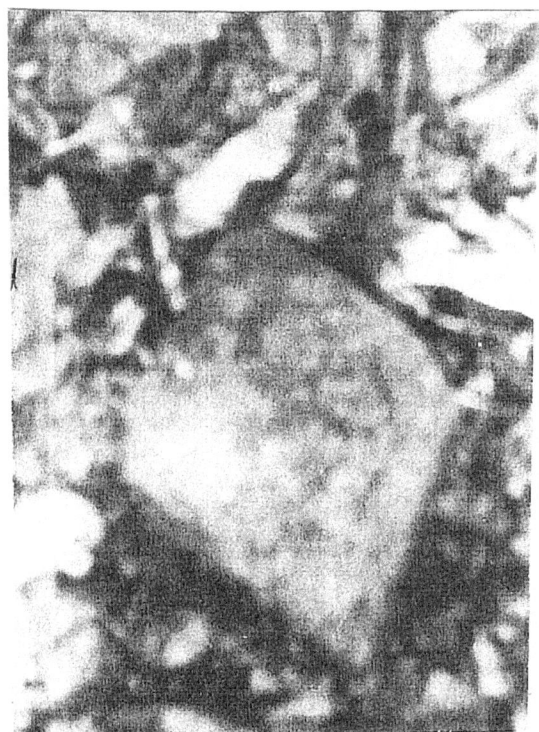
Many think the diamond shaped rocks were copied after the Masonic Lodge Emblem since many KGC members were also Masons.

This is the Masons insignia. Note the resemblance to the diamond shaped rocks.

The author standing next to the "Bible Tree," so named by Bob Brewer for its apparent connections to the Bible.

This is the "Bible Tree." It is very old, and so are the carvings that Bob says contain references to Bible verses that are significant leads to find the treasures.

The author is shown here holding a false grave marker with the name of "Annie E. Spaueding" that had been discovered over a false grave in an old cemetery. It obviously contains a coded message as a key to finding a treasure buried during the 1800's by the Knights the Golden Circle somewhere in the vicinity.

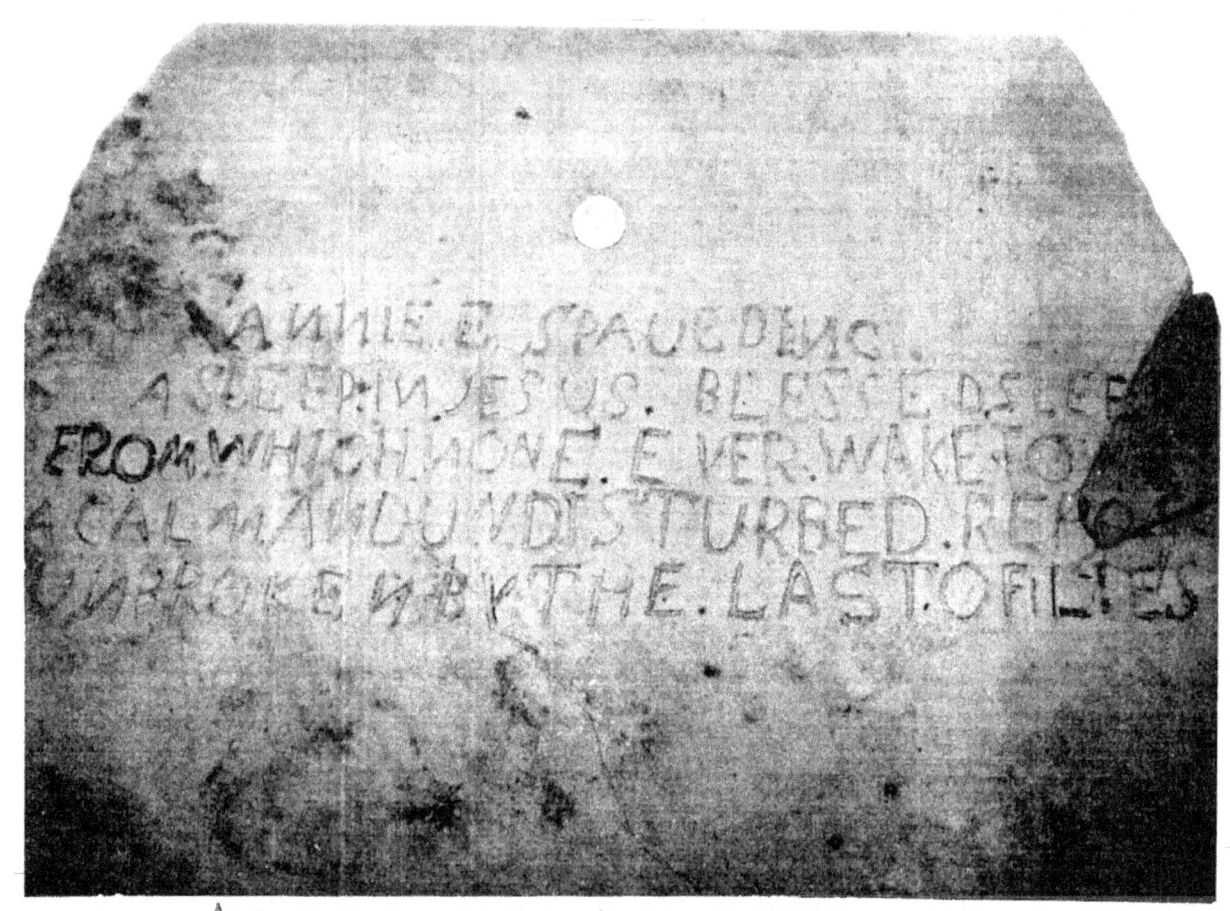

ANNIE..E..SPAUEDING
ASLEEP.IN.JESUS. BLESSED.SLEEP
FROM.WHICH.NONE. EVER.WAKE TO
ACALMANDUNDISTURBED. REPOSE
UNBROKENBY THE.LAST.OF.LIES

Here is a close-up photo of the strange inscriptions on the tombstone, along with a sketch of the wording as near as possible to the exact way it was written. It was meant to appear as done by an uneducated person—but take another good look. The words are a bit puzzling to begin with. Then note the "N's." They are all written backwards except in one case. Why? Also note the strange use of periods—two after *Annie*, two after *E*, two after *sleep* (but one on top of the other), then one also after: *in, Jesus, from, which, none, ever, undisturbed, the,* and *last*. Why? Most of the words on the third line are run together. Why? What are the hidden meanings? Can you figure them out? Was there ever an "Annie E. Spaueding? It was found on a false grave in a graveyard and it gives clues for those who know how to interrupt it to a hidden treasure. False graves were a favorite place for the KGC to hide their treasures since they were not likely to be disturbed.

  (Note the dime on top as a reference to its size.)

Chapter Seven

Was KGC Treasure Buried On My Fathers Old Farm In Kansas?

The morning following our trip with Hillbilly Bob in southwestern Arkansas, John and I said our goodbyes and headed for Wichita Kansas where I was to catch an airplane late that day for my home in Los Angeles. But on the way, I wanted to visit one more time the old farm that had been owned by my grandparents and my father a short distance east of Wichita. It was in a heavily wooded area of the Flint Hills. It was here that I had spent many happy summers all during my grade school years in the 1930s. The farm was remote. It had no electricity, no indoor plumbing, no water, no gas--not even a telephone. It was a throwback to the turn-of-the-century living. But that's how my grandparents had always lived and wanted to keep it that way. They disliked city life.

But to me, it was a wonderful adventure and a great change from the city life that I was normally used to while attending school. It was truly back-to-nature-living with lots of farm animals around. At night, there were sounds of Whippoorwills in the distant woods and coyotes sometimes prowled around close to the house at night, often howling, that made my German shepherd dog very upset. To me, it was a wonderland. I hunting and fished around all of it many times in my young life, and I knew every part of it. But since I had rarely visited it in my adult life and had not seen it at all in over 25 years, I wanted to take advantage of this opportunity to see it one more time as we passed by.

John and I arrived there very early one morning after spending the night nearby. The house and improvements had long been gone, but it brought back a treasure of memories. What I would give if I could live some of them over again. They were some of the happiest times in my life.

While we were visiting a hilltop on my grandparent's old place, we watched six deer come out of the timber to cross over a meadow towards us. But when they spotted us, they ran back into the timber. We also found numerous beaver signs along the creek where we used to fish. There were no deer or beaver around when we lived there, and I was gratified to see wildlife returning to the area.

Then we went down the road about a mile to where my father had owned 80-acres. One reason that I especially wanted to visit it was because I knew that it was located along the old wagon trail where the old wagon trains and caravans had used to make a crossing over a huge, flat rock on a creek that ran through his property. It was the only place for miles around where they could get across easily all-year-round. That had gone on for many years before a road and a bridge was finally established along the side of the property. This had happened a number of years before my dad acquired the property in 1927. However, the old wagon ruts are still plainly visible where they had come out of the woods on the eastern side, crossed the flat rock area that was about the size of a football field, then entered the woods on the other side and continued on Westward. The area was almost like a park. Sometimes, we went there for picnics. On the East side was a large grove of pecan trees that abound in squirrels and rabbits. The stream was clear and full of fish, especially catfish. It was my all-time favorite fishing hole. Horses and cattle could be watered as the stream got very shallow as it flowed over the huge flat rock. It was a great place to swim or take a bath. I know, since I had done so many times.

I knew that it was an ideal place where wagons and caravans could stop and rest for a few days, and obviously they had. So I figured that it was a likely place to find some old relics and maybe some old coins with metal detectors that John and I had. So, we parked along the road, took our metal detectors and cameras and headed in. I was delighted to see that it had not changed a bit in all of those years. It was exactly as I had remembered it. After taking a few pictures, we started searching around with our metal detectors. Before we knew it, we were out a time and had to leave for Wichita or else I would miss my plane. Though we didn't find any coins, we did find a few old relics that might have come from a wagon or a harness.

With me in the lead, I started following an old trail towards the road. Suddenly, I was startled! I had just stepped over a rock that looked exactly like the boot rocks that we had seen in southwestern Arkansas with Bob Brewer.

Now, wait a minute! That was over 450 miles away from here. What would one of these boot rocks be doing up here on my father's old place? I turned around to look again and when I did, I saw three of the diamond-shaped rocks a few feet away, just like the ones we had seen before. I was astonished! Just then, John caught up with me and without looking up or raising my head, I said to John, "Where is the bent tree?"

"What bent tree?" he asked.

I repeated by question again, and he quickly answered, "Well, there's one right there behind you. Why?"

Well," I said, "There must be one, because here is a boot-shaped rock and three diamond rocks...See?"

John was astonished just as I was. We could hardly believe it, but there was no doubt that what we were looking at was identical to the signs that Bob Brewer had shown us before. That could only mean that the KGC had also been active in this area and presumably had buried a treasure on my father's property before he owned it. That seemed awesome to me and I couldn't help thinking that if I had known then what I knew now, there would have been a great treasure hunt going on back then.

I hurriedly took a few pictures of the stones, but ran out of film before I could get one of the bent tree. When we reached the car, I showed John were the old house across the road had been. Only the huge stone chimney was left. We both agreed that this must have been where the KGC sentinel had lived that watched over the treasure site on my father's old property.

THE SENTINEL WHO HAD THREATENED MY GRANDFATHER

Then, we quickly headed for the airport at Wichita, getting there just in time to catch the plane for Los Angeles. Then on the way home, I recalled an incident that happened shortly after my father had purchased the property. My grandfather discovered that the fence around the property did not include a small part of the southeast corner that was bounded on the south side by the road and on the east side by the creek. The area covered approximately four or five acres, which was equivalent to about half the size of a city block. So, when my grandfather went over to take the old fence down and put up a new one to include the corner, he was threatened by a man who lived across the road from it. He said that he would shoot my grandfather if he tried to change the fence.

So, my grandfather waited until spring when my father brought me up for my usual summer visit. Now my father, who was born in Kansas in 1890, had been an old cowboy around Dodge City and had been involved in a shooting scrape, or two, himself, so he was not one to back off from anyone's threat. He immediately let the word out that when we got there, he and my grandfather were going to change the fence, and anybody approaching them with a gun would be shot.

When we arrived, the three of us went over to the property with fencing equipment. My father brought along his 30.30 rifle and his old Colt revolver. My grandfather brought along his old double-barreled shotgun. They kept their weapons handy as they worked, while I played nearby in the woods with my BB gun. The man across the road pretended not to notice. He never made any more threats, nor did he ever attempt to change the fence back.

The reason I am writing about this incident is because I realized while on the airplane that the man who had threatened my grandfather must have been a second, or maybe a third, generation sentinel, and he was only trying to live up to the responsibilities handed down to him. If he had not been a sentinel, then why would he have been interested in the property otherwise, since all his property was across the road and he had not used my dad's property for anything, except to keep everyone away from it.

In conclusion, I have become more convinced than ever, that as improbable as I first thought, there indeed was a secret Confederate organization known as the Knights of the Golden Circle that had numbered into the hundreds of thousands who had been very powerful and influential and who had accumulated a great amount of money and treasure for the purpose of restarting the Civil War, but somehow their plans never worked out…only their treasures still exist.

What I observed and found at Glorieta Pass, New Mexico, then in southwestern Arkansas and Oklahoma, and finally on my father's old farm in Kansas, must lead to a conclusion that not one person, nor even a few people, but dozens of people had been responsible for just what I had personally seen. Surely, there must be many, many more of these clues scattered around the country since I had already witnessed them in four states. They cannot be passed off as a type of graffiti nor the result of the personal hobby of a few people. They have to represent something a lot more than that. Meaning that if they are not treasure signs, what else could they possibly be???

Oh yes, am I going back to look for treasure on my father's old farm? I think the reader should know the answer to that by now.

And remember, when you are out there someplace, if you want to find some treasure, keep a keen eye open for treasure signs. Most of them are not obvious, but they could be anywhere.

NOTICE TO READERS

The author is preparing a follow-on book: "HOW TO FIND THE TREASURES OF THE KNIGHTS OF THE GOLDEN CIRCLE." Most of this important information has been found in past issues of the prestigious "TREASURE HUNTER CONFIDENTIAL" publication. It was top-of-the-line information and privately published from 1989 through 2002. It was intended for the serious treasure hunter by mail order only. It never appeared on any news stands. Subscribers paid $100 a year for 12 issues and most thought it was well worth it. The author and Steve Ryland once served as staff members and news writers. The publication was unique in that it accepted no commercials and therefore not under the influence of any commercial interests. Most of the information was proprietary, very useful and rarely (if ever) found elsewhere.

It was one of the first publications (if not the first) to mention the Knights of the Golden Circle and their treasures. Much intensive research and interviews with historians and professional treasure hunters by Larry

Williams, the originator of the publication, resulted in much informative information. This included overlays for KGC maps, diagrams, locations and treasure signs with their probable meaning, found only there.

Every serious or armchair treasure hunter, including historians, should get a copy. Watch for it soon.

This shows where the old wagon trail crossed a stream over a large flat rock area on an old farm in Kansas that my father owned during the 1920s and 30's. It had been used since the early days of Kansas until a bridge was built nearby in about 1910. It had also been my favorite fishing hole when I was a boy.

This is a close up of the far side of the above photo. Wagon ruts made during the 1800s are still clearly visible. This area had also been a popular stopover location.

As John Melanscon and myself were leaving the site along this trail back to the road, I noticed this boot shaped rock and three diamond shaped rocks exactly like we had seen two days before with Bob Brewer in southwestern Arkansas. There was also a bent tree and nearby.

This is a close up of the man-made stone boot. Compare it with the photo of a stone boot in Chapter Six.

This is an elongated diamond rock.

The underside of the elongated diamond rock shows the KGC validation mark--a corner that has been chiseled away.

A differently shaped rock, so it must have a special meaning.

This big, sturdy, stone chimney is all that remains of the very old house that I remember located across the road from my fathers place in Kansas. It was the oldest house in the area and where the man lived who threatened to shoot my grandfather. Apparently, he was the KGC sentinel who had lived there.

This is a photo of my father, Guy Roush, posing for a picture on his ranch near Lamar, Colorado, before he went out to ride the herd. It was taken a few years before he bought the farm in Kansas. He was born in Kansas and 1890 and was a real life cowboy, bronc buster and rancher in his early life around Dodge City. Later in life, we often went treasure hunting together. He never took threats or abuse from anybody--even a KGC Sentinel.

About the Author, Dr. Roy William Roush, Ph.D.

The author is one of the most recognized names in the world as an authority on the subject of Treasure Hunting and Gold Prospecting for over 40 years. He has also been very active in those fields and has served as a researcher and consultant for a number of organizations and individuals, plus organizing and participating in treasure expeditions and underwater salvage projects in the Florida Keys, the Bahamas, Turks and Caicos Islands, Mexico, Puerto Rico, and Europe, as well as throughout the United States.

Obtaining a B.A. Degree in Journalism in 1950, he used his journalism expertise to write for many of the Treasure Hunting Publications including: "Treasure," "Treasure Hunter," "Treasure Search," "Treasure Found," and "Treasure News." Later, he earned a Ph.D. in Archaeology.

He also fought with the US Marines in World War II during the battles of Guadalcanal, Tarawa, Saipan, and Tinian in the South Pacific as a front-line combat rifleman. Then, during the Korean War, he flew Jet Fighters and F-51 Mustang's as an officer with the U.S. Air Force. Recently, he authored a major book about his experiences in combat and as an Air Force fighter pilot, entitled "OPEN FIRE." (Website OPEN-FIRE.US)

Being one of the first to use a metal detector in the early 1960's (building his first one in 1962), he has searched for many of the well-know lost treasures, including: the Lost Dutchman; the 17 Tons of Mexican Gold in New Mexico; Peg Leg's Black Gold Nuggets; Iron Door Mine; Knights of the Golden Circle Treasures; Vasquez's Bandit Loot; Lost Arch Mine; Black Beard's Treasure; etc.

As an expert with all kinds of metal detectors and has won numerous National Metal Detecting Contests. His collection of items found is impressive. He has taught courses on Treasure Hunting, Ghost Towns and Gold Prospecting at UCLA, Los Angeles City College, the Elks Lodge in Glendale, Keene Engineering, the Treasure Emporium, taught Metal Detecting to the FBI, and is the consultant on Metal Detecting to the Los Angeles City Police Department. Currently, He is featured in the popular commercial video "Prospecting for Gold," available at most Gold Prospecting and Treasure Hunting shops.

He is a popular guest speaker on these subjects to many clubs and organizations, including "The Gene Autry Museum of Western History;" "The Gold Prospectors Association," "The Adventures' Club of Los Angeles," and has himself been the subject of many newspaper and magazine articles, television and radio programs. He has served as technical consultant for numerous treasure publications and television programs--plus featured in some including "Unsolved Mysteries," "The Treasure Hunters," "The Search for Amazing Treasures," Bill Burrud's "Treasure Series," NBC's specials on "Gold Prospecting" and "Treasure Hunting."

He owns one of the largest private libraries on Treasure Hunting in the world that includes thousands of books, magazine and newspaper articles, videos, tapes and photographs.

www.ingramcontent.com/pod-product-compliance
Lightning Source LLC
Chambersburg PA
CBHW060316240426
43661CB00059B/2778